Advances and Applications in Deep Learning

Edited by Marco Antonio Aceves-Fernandez

Published in London, United Kingdom

IntechOpen

Supporting open minds since 2005

Advances and Applications in Deep Learning
http://dx.doi.org/10.5772/intechopen.87786
Edited by Marco Antonio Aceves-Fernandez

Part of IntechOpen Book Series: Artificial Intelligence, Volume 4
Book Series Editor: Marco Antonio Aceves-Fernandez

Contributors
Md Nazmus Saadat, Muhammad Shuaib, Evren Daglarli, Joongheon Kim, Dohyun Kim, Soohyun Park, Andrey Miroshnichenko, Lei Xu, Lujun Huang, Jing He, Wen Xu, Yanfeng Shu, Hui Zheng

First published in London, United Kingdom, 2020 by IntechOpen
IntechOpen is the global imprint of INTECHOPEN LIMITED, registered in England and Wales, registration number: 11086078, 5 Princes Gate Court, London, SW7 2QJ, United Kingdom
Printed in Croatia

British Library Cataloguing-in-Publication Data
A catalogue record for this book is available from the British Library

Additional hard and PDF copies can be obtained from orders@intechopen.com

Advances and Applications in Deep Learning
Edited by Marco Antonio Aceves-Fernandez
p. cm.
Print ISBN 978-1-83962-878-8
Online ISBN 978-1-83962-879-5
eBook (PDF) ISBN 978-1-83962-880-1
ISSN 2633-1403

For EU product safety concerns:
IN TECH d.o.o., Prolaz Marije Krucifikse Kozulić 3, 51000 Rijeka, Croatia, info@intechopen.com or visit our website at intechopen.com.

IntechOpen Book Series
Artificial Intelligence
Volume 4

Dr. Marco A. Aceves-Fernandez obtained his BSc (Eng) in Telematics from the Universidad de Colima, Mexico. He obtained both his MSc and PhD from the University of Liverpool, England, in the field of Intelligent Systems. He is full professor at the Universidad Autonoma de Queretaro, Mexico. He has been a recognized member of the National System of Researchers (SNI) since 2009. He has published more than eighty research papers as well as a number of book chapters and congress papers. He has contributed in more than twenty funded research projects, both academic and industrial, in the area of artificial intelligence, including environmental, biomedical, automotive, aviation, consumer, and robotics applications. He is also honorary president at the Mexican Association of Embedded Systems (AMESE), a senior member of the Institute of Electrical and Electronics Engineer (IEEE), and a board member for many institutions and associations. His research interests include intelligent and embedded systems.

Editor of Volume 4:
Marco A. Aceves-Fernández, Ph.D.
Universidad Autónoma de Querétaro
Faculty of Engineering, Querétaro, México

Book Series Editor: Marco A. Aceves-Fernandez
Universidad Autónoma de Querétaro
Faculty of Engineering, Querétaro, México

Scope of the Series

Artificial Intelligence (AI) is a rapidly developing multidisciplinary research area that aims to solve increasingly complex problems. In today´s highly integrated world, AI promises to become a robust and powerful mean for obtaining solutions to previously unsolvable problems. This book series is intended for researchers and students alike, as well as all those interested in this fascinating field and its applications, in particular in areas related to the topics on which it is focused.

Contents

Preface

Since the earliest humans populated the earth, we have gradually tried to understand and control the world around us. In trying to understand such phenomena, humans began to make predictions to various extents. For instance, humans made predictions about motions of the planets, eclipses, cycles of rainfall, and periodicity of certain diseases. However, in the last few decades, the complexity of these predictions have outpaced our abilities to predict.

Luckily, the dawn of electronic computers is increasing our abilities to predict nature, although the problems we are facing now are far more complex than the problems we faced a century ago.

The ability of machines to demonstrate advanced cognitive skills in taking decisions, learning, perceiving the environment, predicting certain behavior, and processing written or spoken languages, among other skills, makes the discipline of artificial intelligence of paramount importance in today's world.

This book compiles a wide range of applications in Deep Learning in two sections: "Deep Learning Applications" and "Future Trends of Deep Learning."

This work will be of interest to students and researchers alike, as I did my best to comprise quality research contributions with a number of different applications.

Marco A. Aceves-Fernández, Ph.D.
Faculty of Engineering,
Universidad Autónoma de Querétaro,
Querétaro, México

Section 1

Deep Learning Applications

Chapter 1

Advancements in Deep Learning Theory and Applications: Perspective in 2020 and beyond

Md Nazmus Saadat and Muhammad Shuaib

Abstract

The aim of this chapter is to introduce newcomers to deep learning, deep learning platforms, algorithms, applications, and open-source datasets. This chapter will give you a broad overview of the term deep learning, in context to deep learning machine learning, and Artificial Intelligence (AI) is also introduced. In Introduction, there is a brief overview of the research achievements of deep learning. After Introduction, a brief history of deep learning has been also discussed. The history started from a famous scientist called Allen Turing (1951) to 2020. In the start of a chapter after Introduction, there are some commonly used terminologies, which are used in deep learning. The main focus is on the most recent applications, the most commonly used algorithms, modern platforms, and relevant open-source databases or datasets available online. While discussing the most recent applications and platforms of deep learning, their scope in future is also discussed. Future research directions are discussed in applications and platforms. The natural language processing and auto-pilot vehicles were considered the state-of-the-art application, and these applications still need a good portion of further research. Any reader from undergraduate and postgraduate students, data scientist, and researchers would be benefitted from this.

Keywords: deep learning, machine learning, artificial intelligence, neural networks

1. Introduction

Deep learning is focusing comprehensively on video, image, text and audio recognition, autonomous driving, robotics, healthcare, etc. [1]. Deep learning is a result orientated field of study that why getting very much attention from researcher and academicians. The Rina Dechter introduced the word of deep learning in 1986, the main motivation behind the advent of field deep learning was making an intelligent machine that mimic the human brain. In humans, the brain is the most important and decision-making organ; brain takes decision based on sight, smell, touch, and sounds. The brain also can store memory and solve complex problems based on their experience.

For the last few decades, the researchers dreamed of making a machine that is as intelligent as, like our brains, they started studying the biological structure and working of the human brain. Making a robot that performs certain duties and self-driving cars is to reduce roadside incidents. Because according to the World

Health Organization (WHO), 1.35 million people die every year in road incidents [2] and approximately 90% of the incidents are due to human errors [3]. To develop state-of-the-art devices for the applications listed above, ones need to think in a different way of programming a device to make it artificially intelligent. Deep learning is one of the most innovative paradigms that make it possible up to some extent. In deep learning, the word deep indicates the number of layers through which data are converted from input to the desired output. It is difficult for a new researcher or student to recognize any project whether it is from artificial intelligence machine learning or deep learning because all these overlap each other some way or the other. Machine learning is any sort of computer program that can learn by their own without having specially programmed by the programmer. There are two types of machine learning: supervised learning and unsupervised learning. In supervised learning, you teach or train the machine with a fully labeled data, the machine learns from the labeled data and then anticipate the unforeseen data. In supervised learning, the machine can only give you correct output when the input is already experienced in training phase; it is based on experience; the more is the training dataset or experience of your machine the higher is the chances of getting the actual output. It is a time-consuming process and also required a lot of expertise in data science. On the other hand, in unsupervised learning, supervision of a model is not needed, rather the model work on its own catches new data and discovers the information inside the data. It usually deals with label-less data; compared to supervised learning, unsupervised learning is more complicated. It is usually used to find features and unknown patterns.

Deep learning models are agile and result oriented in terms of complicated abstractions. Deep learning models are mostly based on ANN, categorically CNNs, although there are deep belief networks, generative models, propositional formulas and Boltzmann machine also play their part (**Figure 1**).

Deep learning has been evaluated as a game-changer in AI and computer vision. Today, state-of-the-art object detection is possible only due to deep learning [4]; traditional methods of object detection are not enough to cater with detection so smartly. To understand the whole image of object detection, it is not necessary

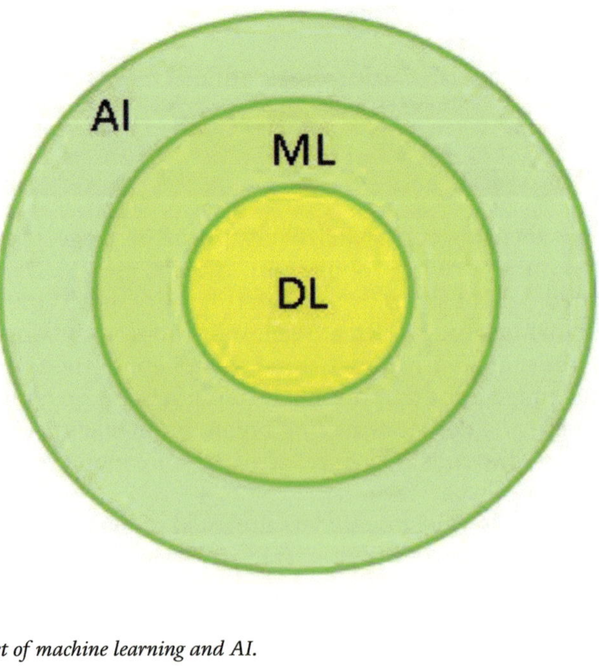

Figure 1.
Deep learning a subset of machine learning and AI.

to only focus on image classification, but to precisely calculate the concept and locations of the objects in every image, that is, object detection which is based on face detection, pedestrian detection, and skeleton detection [5]. Deep learning has cutting-edge technology and has application in every field of life ranging from computational to healthcare. It has a very deep impact on the life of the people or societies because its application is always the need of the day. The deep learning also gains significant importance due to new and flourishing field called big data analytics. Big data analytics is the number of complicated processes examining large and varied data sets, or it is also defined as techniques and methods used to identify the hidden patterns, unknown correlations market trends, and customer preference from huge dataset. Big data analytics can offer various business benefits, that is, more effective marketing strategies, better customer service, improved operational efficiency, etc.

Deep learning is an emerging area of research and modern application. The deep learning is a very widespread and demanding field now-days, it covers industry, business, and healthcare; it combines all the hot research-oriented fields, that is, IoT, e-health-care, cybersecurity, bioinformatics, optimization, and cyber-physical systems; these all are seen interdependent. Gartner has proposed top ten technology trends for 2020, some of them are, hyper-automation, human augmentation, AI Security, IoT, Autonomous things; etc.; all are related to AI, machine learning, and deep learning some way or the other. Surely, deep learning will bring a bunch of innovations to everywhere whether it is industry, health-care or business intelligence. According to Ref. [6], machine learning and AI will be used more in 2020 experts says in the survey conducted by the computer-world.

In 2019, many researchers, academicians, and teachers claimed that deep learning is over because it cannot do common-sense reasoning; Rodney Brooks a professor in MIT says that some popular press started stories that the deep learning will be over by 2020. In 2020, hybrid, interdisciplinary, collaborative, and open-minded research is expected to add more contribution. The topics that are expected to be more prevalent in 2020 are common-sense reasoning, active learning and life-long learning, multi-modal and multi-task learning, open-domain dialogue conversation, medical applications and autonomous vehicles, ethics that includes privacy, confidentiality, and biases, and finally robotics.

There are two most common deep learning platforms: TensorFlow and PyTorch; these two platforms compete; and this competition is very fruitful for the community; TensorFlow is easy to use, integrated with Keras; while on the other hand, Pytorch has TPU support, etc. In 2020, it is expected to have a platform which can easily transform a TensorFlow model to Pytorch and vice versa. There is a need to develop an actively developed stable reinforcement learning framework. The higher layers of abstractions are expected in 2020 like Keras, so that machine learning is used outside the machine learning fields.

1.1 History

Deep learning is a sub branch of machine learning, and machine learning is a sub branch of artificial intelligence. Deep learning is a set of algorithms that processes large set of data and imitates the thinking process. The history of deep leaning is started from 1943, when Warren McCulloch and Walter Pitts created a neural network-based computer model. There basic aim was to mimic thought process of human brain; they used algorithms and mathematics to make the threshold logic to mimic human thought process. Alan Turing called the father of AI concluded in 1951 that the machines would not take much time in started thinking of their own; at some point of time, they would be able to talk to each other; and it is also expected that they would take the control of the universe. In context to this, the frank Rosenblatt introduced single and multi-layer artificial neural network (1957–1962). The history amazed us when the world champion of chess player called Kasparov was defeated by Deep blue computer in 1997. In 1957–62, the single layer and multi-layer perceptron's was introduced. The first deep feedforward general purpose learning algorithm multilayer perceptron's by Alexey Icakhnenko and Lapa was published in 1967. In 1971, a deep network with eight layers trained by the group method of data handling algorithm was described already. The idea of backpropagation, Recurrent Neural Network (RNN), and restricted Boltzmann machine (RBM) was introduced in 1970–1986. In 1979-1998, the Convolution Neural Network (CNN), Bidirectional RNN, and long short-term memory (LSTM) were the state of the art. The deep belief network (DBN) was introduced by Geoff Hinton in 2006. The data sets called ImageNet and AlexNet that was created in 2009. Generative Adversarial Network (GAN) is a class of machine learning system invented by Ian Goodfellow and his colleagues in 2014. Coming up in history in 2016 Google DeepMind challenge match between Alpha Go versus Lee Sedol, the AlphaGo win all the matches from a world champion Lee Sedol. AlfaGo and AlfaZero are computer programs developed by artificial intelligence research company called DeepMind in (2016–2017); it plays the board game Go. The transformer introduced in 2017–19 a deep learning model used specially used for Natural language Processing (NLP). Although there is a lot of community contributed to the deep learning but Yann LeCun, Geoffrey Hinton, and Yoshua Bengio have received Turing awards in 2018.

2. Deep network topologies

2.1 Deep neural network (DNN)

In DNN, there is multilayer perceptron or hidden layer between the input and output. All the layers are connected to previous layers; by going through each layer, the network estimates the exact output based on the weights and activation function. Through DNN, we can model any complex non-linear relation. The backbone of the DNN is the characteristic of learning about the feature that is most relevant to the targets [7]. The DNN has research gap in model selection, training dynamics, by using graph convolution neural network combination optimization, and Bayesian neural network for estimation of uncertainty. There are a lot of applications for DNN, that is, computer vision, machine translation, social network filtering, playing board, video games, and medical diagnosis (**Figure 2**).

2.2 Recurrent neural network (RNN)

RNN is a type of deep learning network that is used specifically when there is sequential data or time-series, that is, video, speech, etc. The RNN usually maintained the data from the previous state to the next state. It is called recurrent because it performs the same function for each input, while the output is different because it also depends on past calculations. The state-of-the-art topic of deep learning with RNN is Long Short-Term Memory Network (LSTM). RNN provides the solution to many problems, that is, intelligent transportation system [8], solving time-varying matrix inversion [9], and many more. The RNN is famous for sentence evaluation and linguistic data processing (**Figure 3**).

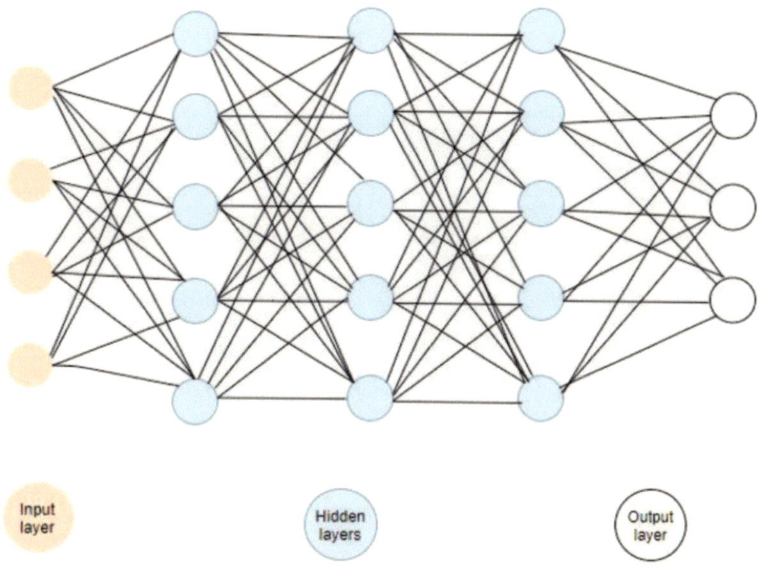

Figure 2.
Deep neural network.

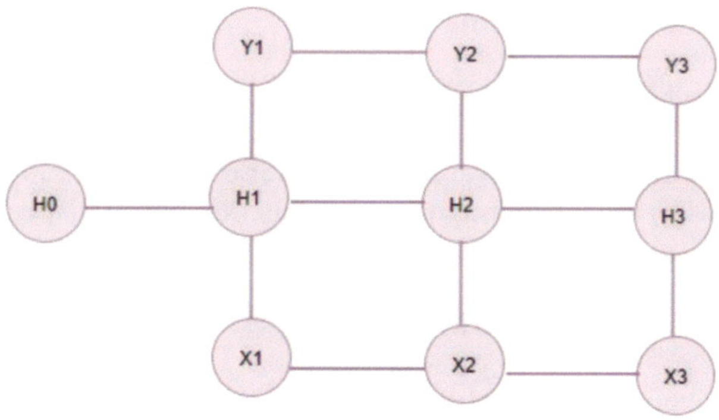

Figure 3.
Recurrent neural network.

2.3 Deep belief network (DBN)

DBN is a probabilistic unsupervised deep learning algorithm. It has many layers of hidden variables. To solve the more complex problems, it needs more hidden layers; each layer is a special statistical relation with the other layer. DBN can learn probabilistically; after learning, BDN needs training under supervisor to perform classification. The DBN is used to recognize clusters and generates images, video sequences, and motion-capture data (**Figure 4**).

2.4 Boltzmann machine (BM)

The BM is a network that is a uniformly attached, neuron-like unit, which is responsible for taking decisions stochastically about whether to be off or on. Computational problems are solved through BM like search, optimization, and learning problem. Many features are uncovered in learning algorithm that shows

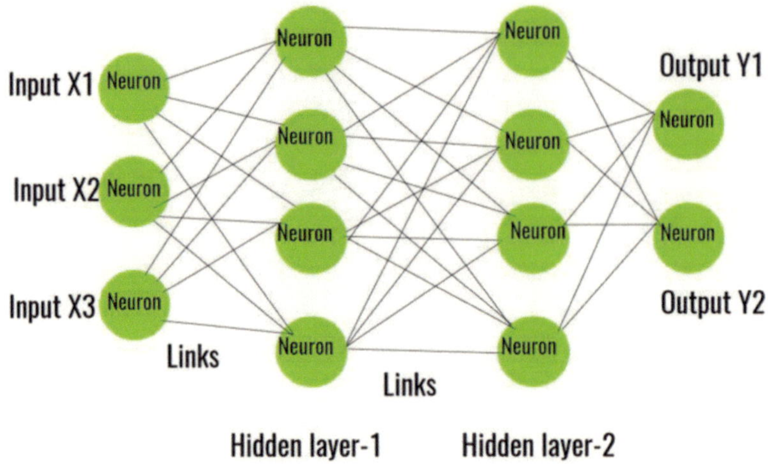

Figure 4.
Deep belief network.

very complex behavior in training dataset. Boltzmann machine is used for classification and dimensionality reduction.

2.5 Restricted Boltzmann machine (RBM)

RBM introduced in 1986 by Smolensky: two layers visible and hidden units, while there is no connection between visible-visible and hidden-hidden. It can learn a probability distribution over a collection of datasets. The applications of RBM are features learning, collaborative filtering, dimensionality reduction, and classification.

2.6 Convolutional neural network (CNN)

In CNN, the layers are delicately connected to input layer as well as each other. There is a specific function for each neuron of the subsequent layer like it is only responsible for only a part of the input. CNN is now widely used for remote sensing, computer vision, audio, and text processing [10].

2.7 Deep auto-encoder

Just like others, deep auto-encoder has also many hidden layers. The difference between a simple auto-encoder and deep-auto-encoder is the simple auto-encoder that has one hidden layer, while the deep-auto-encoder has many hidden layers. In deep-auto-encoder, the training is complex normally, you need to train one hidden layer first to reconstruct the structure of the input data, and this input data are further used to train other hidden layers and so on. Some applications of deep auto-encoder are image extraction, image generation recommendation system, and sequence to sequence prediction.

2.8 Gradient descent (GD)

GD is used to reduce the overall cost function; it is considered as an optimization algorithm and is widely used for determination of coefficient function in machine learning. When there is not possible to estimate the parameters analytically, then

GD is used to calculate the desired parameters. Using the GD weight of the model is updated for every epoch. It is used for supervised machine learning.

2.9 Stochastic gradient descent (SGD)

Just like GD, SGD is also an optimization algorithm but GD is used when the datasets are small, while SGD is usually used when the datasets are large, and SD becomes very costly if used for a large number of datasets.

3. Application of deep learning

Deep learning is new and state-of-the-art technology used for large scale applications now-days. Deep learning (also called differential programming or structure learning) is member of a large family of machine learning class. It is edge-cutting technology used for many different new research fields which are stated below.

3.1 Deep learning in automatic speech recognition

The automatic speech recognition is the convincing application of deep learning. Speech recognition means making speech as in input to a machine that can make the input process very easy and has a hundred of other advantages as well, that is, illiterate people can also use technology, speech coding, text to speech synthesis, speech recognition, speaker recognition, speech enhancement, speech segmentation, language identification, and many more [11]. The speech is the natural form of communication, hence it is considered a very convincing application.

3.2 Image recognition

Image recognition based on deep learning becomes very famous and accurate result-oriented technology based on the training and experience of machine. Deep learning plays a very important part in image recognition and image classification in underwater target recognition [12] although the images from underwater are always noisy and deteriorated. MNIST is one of the most renowned examples used for image classification, below is the simple of dataset of MNIST dataset (**Figure 5**).

3.3 Natural language processing

LSTM helps a lot in language modeling and machine translation [13]; language modeling task is to understand the language. To implement the language, models' neural networks are used. Google translate is the most famous and widely used application in this regard; Google translate is used for more than 100 languages all over the world. It also used LSTM; and it learns from millions of examples and translates the whole sentence rather than word by word translation. BERT (Google) is one of the most common technologies in this field achieved a lot of benchmarks, that is, sentence classification, sentence pair classification, sentence pair similarity, sentence tagging, create contextualized words embedding, question answering, and multiple-choice questions. There are some other transformer-based language models developed in 2019, which are XLNet (Google/CMU), RoBERTa (Facebook), Distil BERT (hugging Face), CTRL (Salesforce), GPT-2 (Open-AI), ALBERT (Google), and Magatron (NVIDIA). Magatron is the largest transformer model ever trained. It has 8.3 million parameters transformer language model. XLNet is the best transformer in terms of performance; XLNet outperforms BERT on 20 tasks

Figure 5.
Image example of handwritten digits from the MNIST dataset.

often by a large margin. ALBERT developed by Google is used to reduce the parameters via cross-layer parameters sharing. The state of the artwork in this domain is about multi-domain task-oriented dialogue system [14]. In 2020, it expected to combine common sense reasoning with language models, extending language model context to thousands of words and to have more focus on open-domain dialogue (**Figure 6**).

3.4 Games and robotics

Robots are the agents who are artificially intelligent and working in the real-world replacing humans. OpenAI and Dota 2 are popular games; in 2017, 1v1 bot beats top professional Dota 2 players; in 2018, OpenAI five lost two games against top Dota 2 player, while in 2019, OpenAI five beat OG team (the world champion in 2018). The OpenAI five win in 2019 is only because of the more training compute; the current version of OpenAI has consumed 800 petaflops/day and experiences about 45,000 years of dota self-play over 10 real-time months. The current version has 99.9%-win rate versus the 2018 version. It is one of the best experiences in deep learning that systems that learn to play with each other and incrementally

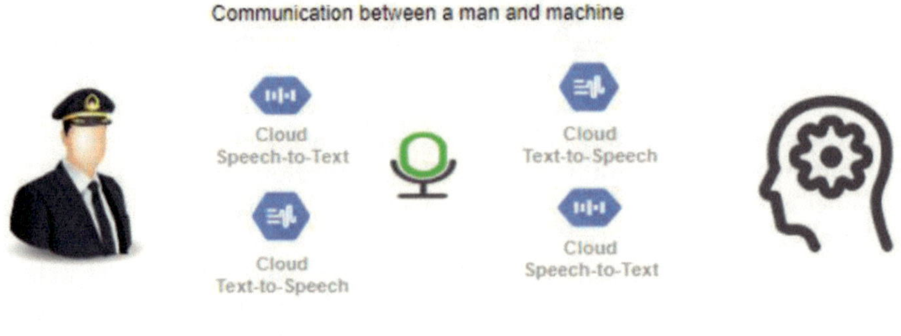

Figure 6.
NLP and deep learning.

improving. OpenAI Rubiks Cube Manipulation is another example from Robotics. The researchers are expecting in 2020 to implement reinforcement-learning methods in the manipulation of real-world interaction tasks. In games, experts are loss from different machines, using these machines to assist human experts in discovering new strategies. Waymo a company that is focusing on developing auto-pilot like Tesla in October 2018; they have 10 million miles on road and now in 2020 they have 20 million miles on road 20,000 of classes for structure test, also initiated testing without having a safety driver.

3.5 Financial fraud detection

Deep learning is playing a very important role in financial fraud detection. With the advent of technology and a significant amount of e-commerce platforms, the number of e-payments is increasing day by day chances of financial fraud, which is also a source of headache for banks and other financial institutions. Thus, focusing on fraud detection is a hot area of research. The author of [15] used auto-encoder for financial fraud detection [16]. This research uses deep learning model for fraud detection, while [17] proposed a solution to fraud detection using machine learning approach.

3.6 Deep learning in health-care

In this modern era of computing, deep learning also produced best results medical and health care, that is, deep learning is used for cancer cell coordination, organ segmentation, protein folding, lesion detection, and image enhancement in the field of medicine. There are several other issues like [18–21] and much more where deep learning is directly involved in the suggestion of the ultimate solution to the problem in healthcare.

3.7 Military

Deep learning is used for making many different military devices used in wars or other spy services. The military is also working on robots to train the robots to handle the critical situation through these robots. The militaries of some countries are making their weapons more intelligent using AI. In a war zone, AI can be embedded in the robots for remote surgical support in healthcare.

3.8 Cybersecurity

Cybersecurity is also one of the hot research areas; deep learning models are used for the cybersecurity of the Internet of Things (IoT) [22]. The IoT devices are usually low power devices having power-constrained that's why always vulnerable to external threats. Deep learning models can detect threats more accurately than any other technology. The author of [23] used deep learning and machine learning for intrusion, spam, and malware detection.

4. Modern deep learning platforms

Open-sources deep learning platforms discussed in this section. It will provide a quick review of the open-source platforms for beginners and mediocre because every platform has its pros and cons.

4.1 TensorFlow

The TensorFlow is new and open-source platform for differential programming; it was developed by Google team called Google brain and was first released in 2015 [24]. In February 2017, they released version 1.0.0; TensorFlow can work on CPU and GPU; it is available for Mac, Linux, and windows and also for mobile computing platform android and iOS. It is the most famous machine learning library in the world today. Its best-supported client language is python but there is also interface available in C++, Java, and GO. It is easy to use and have Keras integration. TensorFlow has many of its versions available like for mobiles TensorFlow lite, for industry TensorFlow Serving, etc.

4.2 Pytorch

Pytorch is also machine learning and deep learning library, based on torch library. It was initially released by Facebook's AI Research lab (FAIR) in 2016. Pytorch has two high-level features, Tensor computing with graphics processing units (GPU), and auto-diff based deep neural network. It is too easy in Pytorch to move tensors to and from GPU. Pytorch Mobile is the version of Pytorch used for mobiles. There are some key features of Pytorch; the first feature is called imperative programming; most of the python code is imperative; this type of programming is more flexible. The other feature of Pytorch is dynamic computation graphs, it run time the system generates the graph structure, dynamic graph work well for dynamic networks like RNN, dynamic graph also makes debugging very easy. The Pytorch provides maximum flexibility and speed during implementing and building deep neural network.

4.3 Theano

Theano is designed by Montreal Institute for Learning Algorithms (MILA), which is very famous after their deployment, but unfortunately, there is no support after version 1.0.0 (November 2017). It is a python library designed for code compilation optimization [25]; it is primarily used for mathematical operations like multi-dimensional arrays. Theano was far better than other python libraries like Numpy in terms of speed, computing symbolic graphs, and stability optimizations. Tensor operations, GPU computation, and parallelism are also supported by Theano.

4.4 Microsoft cognitive toolkit (CNTK)

CNTK is used for commercial-grade distributed deep learning. It can be used as a standalone tool for machine learning or also can be included as a library in C++ programs, python, and C#; its model evaluation functionality can be also used from Java programs. It supports ONNX that allows sharing model with frameworks Caffe2, MXNet, and PyTorch [26]. CNTK can be used only on Linux and Windows. The CNTK is considered as a powerful machine learning platform similar surge of performance as compared to other widely used platforms [27].

4.5 Keras

Keras is a powerful library written in python; it uses TensorFlow, Theano, and CNTK as a framework because it does not have their framework. Keras can work on GPUs and CPUs and can also support RNNs and CNNs. The beauty of Keras is it has the ability of fast and easy prototyping; Keras is user-friendly. It has been ranged one of the most cited API in 2018 and has enough number of users on board.

4.6 Deep learning 4J

It is distributed open-source, robust deep learning framework for Java designed by Skymind [28] which is added a lot to Java ecosystem and eclipse foundation. It has compatibility with Clojure and Scala APIs just like Keras; it is also able to work with both CPUs and GPUs. It is widely used for academics and industrial applications.

4.7 Torch

It is a scientific computing open-source machine learning framework released in October 2002; it is not able to work on CPUs; it is only made to focus on GPUs accelerated computing. It is developed in programming language C and based on Lua, a contribute in a LuaJIT, a scripting language. Max OSX and Ubuntu 12+ can use this framework, although they have Platform for Windows, but their implementations are not supported officially [29].

4.8 Caffe and Caffe2

CAFFE (Convolutional Architecture for Fast Feature Embedding) created by Berkeley AI Research (BAIR) is a framework for deep learning. It is developed in C++ with a python interface. Caffe2 was introduced by the research group of Facebook in 2017, but Caffe2 was merged in PyTorch in March 2018. It supports multiple platforms, that is, Mac OS X, Windows, Linux, iOS, and Android [30].

4.9 Apache MXNet

An MXNet is a fast-scalable deep learning platform that supports many programming languages, i.e., Scala, Julia, C++, R, Python, Gluon API, and Perl APIs. Like Torch, it is also made only for GPUs, and it is very competent in multi GPUs implementations. The Apache MXNet is scalable flexible and portable, and due to these qualities, it attracts many users.

5. Training algorithms

One of the most important parts of deep learning is learning algorithms. The deep neural network can be differentiated only through the number of layers; if the number of layers increases, the network becomes deeper and more complex. Each layer has its specific function or can detect or help in the detection of the special feature.

According to the author [31], if the problem is face recognition, the first layer has the responsibility to recognize edges, the second has to detect higher features such as the nose, eye, ears, etc., the next layer can further dig out the features, and so on. Thus, each layer is developed earlier to the development of training algorithm like gradient descent; that's why these kinds of classifiers are not suitable for a dataset with huge volume or variation. This was discussed by Yann et al. [32]; they further concluded that a system with less manual and more automatic design can give better results in pattern recognition.

Backpropagation is the solution; it takes information from the data without going through classifiers and finds the representation needed for recognition. List of few famous training algorithms is listed below.

5.1 Gradient descent

In statistics, data science, and machine learning, we optimize a lot of stuffs; when we fit a line with linear regression, we optimize the intercept and slope; when we use logistic regression, we optimize a squiggle; when we use t-SNE, we optimize clusters. The gradient descent is used to optimize all these and tons of others as well.

Gradient descent algorithm is similar to Newton's roots finding algorithm of 2D function. The methodology is very simple; just pick a point randomly on a curve and move toward the right or left along x-axis depending on the positive and negative value of the slope of the function at the given point up-till the value of y-axis, that is, function or f(x) becomes zero. There is the same concept behind the gradient descent; we move or traverse along a specific path in many-dimensional space weight when the error rate is reduced to your limits than we stop. It is one of the underlying concepts for most of deep learning and machine learning algorithms.

$$C = \frac{1}{2}(Yexpected - Yactual)^2 \tag{1}$$

5.2 Stochastic gradient descent

A method used for optimizing an objective function with the iterative method is called stochastic gradient descent. It can also be called gradient descent optimization. Stochastic gradient descent would randomly pick one sample for each step and from that, just use this one sample to calculate the derivatives, thus in super sample example, stochastic gradient descent reduced the number of terms by computed by 3.

If we had one million samples than the stochastic gradient descent would reduce the number of terms by computed by factor of one million. In stochastic gradient descent, when minibatch of the number of samples finished running than updates are applied, in here update of weights is more frequent, so we reach a global minimum in less time (**Figure 7**).

Figure 7.
Comparison of GD and SGD.

5.3 Momentum

In stochastic gradient descent to update the weight or to calculate step size, a fixed multiplier is used as a learning rate; this can cause the update to overshoot a potential-minima; if the gradient is too steep or delay, the convergence of the gradient is noisy. The concept of momentum used in Physics is velocity exponentially decreasing an average of gradient [33]. This prevents the descent going in the wrong direction.

5.4 Levenberg-Marquardt algorithm

This type of algorithm is used for curve fitting or non-linear least-squares problems. This algorithm is also called as deep least-square; these kinds of issues arise usually in the least-squares curve fitting. It was first introduced by Kenneth Levenberg in 1944, although it was rediscovered by statistician called Donald Marquardt in 1963.

5.5 Backpropagation through time

It is one of the famous and standard methods used to train the recurrent neural network. It was developed independently by several researchers. Unlike general-purpose optimization techniques, it is faster in training RNN. The backpropagation through time also has issues with local optima [34].

6. Routine challenges of deep learning

According to Google trends graph more and more expert and professionals have attracted toward deep learning in last five year; the percentage of professionals increased from 12 to 100% [35, 36]. Deep learning is used everywhere, that is, bio-informatics, computer vision, IoT security, health-care, e-commerce, digital marketing, natural language processing, and many more [37, 38]. Because of the very hot research area, there must have some challenges which are enlisted below.

6.1 Non-contributing columns or inputs

When dealing with data or making a model, several inputs are not necessary for finding any feature, so it is advised to drop un-necessary attributes. There is also necessary to find one best column and make it separate from the dataset; it can be done using numpy array in Keras; but it is difficult and challenging to find best match attribute.

6.2 Number of hidden layers

The number of hidden layers is directly propositional to computational complexity and deepness of the network. To deal with a large number of layers require a high computational cost, difficult to manage a large number of neurons.

6.3 Optimization algorithms

In model optimizations, gradient descent optimizer helps to make the model cost minimum by adjusting the value; choosing an optimizer is also a challenging task to do, because sometimes it makes your cost of model high rather than decreasing the model cost.

6.4 Loss function

Is from the name indicate loss function, it estimates the loss or the difference between the expected outcome and the actual outcome the formula for loss function is listed below.

$$\text{Floss} = \text{Expected outcome} - \text{actual outcome} \tag{2}$$

There are many different ways to calculate the loss function; choosing a loss function is also one of the essential and challenging tasks of deep learning

6.5 Activation function

There are many different activation functions; every activation function does not produce the same results; sigmoid activation function shows good results with binary classification problem. One needs to be careful about Tanh activation function because of the vanishing gradient problem. In multi-labeled classification, softmax is the best option; Relu should be used when there is much zeros in the input side because Relu is good in dead neuron generation. It is also a point to use the required activation function.

6.6 Epoch

When the dataset is passed backwards and forward through the whole neural network, it is called one epoch, as after every epoch value of weights assigned is analyzed to make model. The weights are changed, checked, and tested in every cycle for the same dataset simulation. The main memory is keeping the record of all the training data; sometimes it is not possible to keep all the record in main memory, like for larger datasets, so the epoch is brought to memory in divided or batches form, and finally the result is represented as an epoch output. Dealing with epoch is also a challenging task in deep learning.

7. Available open-source datasets

Research in machine learning and deep learning is started since last many decades hence significant improvement it brings to the society in terms of various application-based on deep learning and machine learning. There are many freely available datasets on the web which can be used by researchers for various purposes.

Image datasets (Table 1):

Pascal VOC	MS COCO
MNIST handwritten digits	NORB
CIFAR10/CIFAR100 color images data set with	COIL100
Caltech101	Google's Open Images
Caltech 256	COIL 20
The dataset of street view	LabelMe
STL-10	ImageNet

Table 1.
Open source image datasets.

Geospatial datasets available online:

1. NEXRAD

2. OpenstreetMAP

3. Landsat8

Dataset available for text (Table 2):

Google books Ngrams	**Yelp open dataset**	**20 newsgroups**	
UCI's Spambase (Older)	Prediction	UCI machine learning repository	Text classification datasets
SQuAD	Google books Ngrams	Broadcast news	WikiText
Penn Treebank	Reuters news dataset	Billion words dataset:	Common crawl

Table 2.
Text open-source datasets.

Artificial datasets:

1. Arcade Universe

2. Dataset inspired from baby-AIschool

3. All images and question datasets

4. Deep vs. shallow comparison ICML

5. Background correlation

6. Rectangles data

7. Mnist variations

Facial datasets (Table 3):

Labeled faces in the wild	**UMD faces annotated dataset**	**CASIA WebFace facial**
MS-Celeb-1M	Olivetti	Multi-Pie
JACFEE	FERET	mmifacedb
Indian face database	The Yale face database	Mut1nyFace/head segmentation dataset

Table 3.
Databases for face recognitions.

Recent additions of datasets (Table 4):

Open data monitor	Quandl data portal	Mutiny face/head segmentation dataset
Awesome public dataset	Head CT scan dataset	Open datasets
WAPo	Chess dataset	NLP datasets
The UZH-FPV drone racing dataset	**North Korean missile test database**	**Flickr-Faces-HQ Dataset (FFHQ)**
Hotels-50K	MIMIC-CXR	Google Audioset
Two new evaluation data-sets	Open-source biometric data recognition	Uber 2B trip data
Yelp Open Dataset	Core50	Data portals

Table 4.
Free databases developed recently.

Video datasets:

For video only one and big and diverse labeled dataset available is Youtube-8M [39].

Author details

Md Nazmus Saadat* and Muhammad Shuaib
University of Kuala Lumpur, Malaysia

*Address all correspondence to: mdnazmus@unikl.edu.my

References

[1] Aliper A, Plis S, Artemov A, Ulloa A, Mamoshina P, Zhavoronkov A. Deep learning applications for predicting pharmacological properties of drugs and drug repurposing using transcriptomic data. Molecular Pharmaceutics. 2016;**13**(7):2524-2530

[2] World Health Organization. Global status report on road safety. Available from: https://www.who.int/violence_injury_prevention/road_safety_status/2018/en/ [Accessed: 31 Janaury 2018]

[3] U. D. O. Transportation. Critical Reasons for Crashes Investigated in the National Motor Vehicle Crash Causation Survey. Washington, DC: National Center for Statistics and Analysis; 2015

[4] Zhao Z-Q, Zheng P, Xu S-T, Wu X. Object detection with deep learning: A review. IEEE Transactions on Neural Networks and Learning Systems. 2019;**30**(11):3212-3232

[5] Kobatake H, Yoshinaga Y. Detection of spicules on mammogram based on skeleton analysis. IEEE Transactions on Medical Imaging. 1996;**15**(3):235-245

[6] Top 3 enterprise tech trends to watch in 2020. 2020. Available from: https://www.computerworld.com/article/3512109/top-3-enterprise-tech-trends-to-watch-in-2020.html

[7] Zhong S, Hu J, Fan X, Yu X, Zhang H. A deep neural network combined with molecular fingerprints (DNN-MF) to develop predictive models for hydroxyl radical rate constants of water contaminants. Journal of Hazardous Materials. 2020;**383**(5)

[8] Kong J, Huang J, Yu H, Deng H, Gong J, Chen H. RNN-based default logic for route planning in urban environments. Neurocomputing. 2019;**338**:307-320

[9] Zhang Z, Zheng L, Wang M. An exponential-enhanced-type varying-parameter RNN for solving time-varying matrix inversion. Neurocomputing. 2019;**338**:126-138

[10] Konstantinidis D, Argyriou V, Stathaki T. A modular CNN-based building detector for remote sensing images. Computer Networks. 2020;**138**:107034

[11] Karpagavalli S, Chandra EH. A Review on Automatic Speech Recognition Architecture and Approaches. International Journal of Signal Processing, Image Processing and Pattern Recognition. 2016;**9**(4):393-404

[12] Jin L, Liang H. Deep Learning for Underwater Image Recognition in Small Sample Size Situations. Aberdeen UK: OCEANS; 2017

[13] Jozefowicz R, Vinyals O, Schuster M, Shazeer N, Wu Y. Exploring the Limits of Language Modeling. California, USA: Google Brain; 2016

[14] Wu CS, Madotto A, Hosseini-Asl E, Xiong C, Socher R, Fung P. Transformable multi domain state generator for task oriented dialogue system. In: arXiv preprint arXiv; 2019

[15] Zamini M, Montazer G. Credit Card Fraud Detection using autoencoder based clustering. In: 9th International Symposium on Telecommunications (IST). Tehran, Iran; 2018. pp. 486-491

[16] Mubalaike AM, Adali E. Deep learning approach for intelligent financial fraud detection system. In: 3rd International Conference on Computer Science and Engineering (UBMK). Sarajevo, Bosnia; 2018

[17] Vidanelag HMMH, Tasnavijitvong T, Suwimonsatein P, Meesad P. Study on machine learning

techniques with conventional tools for payment fraud detection. In: 11th International Conference on Information Technology and Electrical Engineering (ICITEE). Pattaya, Thailand; 2019

[18] Subiksha K. Improvement in analyzing healthcare systems using deep learning architecture. In: 4th International Conference on Computing Communication and Automation (ICCCA). Greater Noida, India; 2018

[19] Hajjo R. The ethical challenges of applying machine learning and artificial intelligence in cancer care. In: 1st International Conference on Cancer Care Informatics (CCI). Amman, Jordan; 2018

[20] Nugroho H, Harmanto D, Hassan Al-Absi HR. On the development of smart home care: Application of deep learning for pain detection. In: IEEE-EMBS Conference on Biomedical Engineering and Sciences (IECBES). Sarawak, Malaysia; 2018

[21] Shickel B, Tighe PJ, Bihorac A, Rashidi P. Deep EHR: A survey of recent advances in deep learning techniques for electronic health record (EHR) analysis. IEEE Journal of Biomedical and Health Informatics. 2017;**22**(5):1589-1604

[22] Roopak M, Tian GY, Chambers J. Deep learning models for cyber security in IoT networks. In: IEEE 9th Annual Computing and Communication Workshop and Conference (CCWC). Las Vegas USA; 2019

[23] Apruzzese G, Colajanni M, Ferretti L, Guido A, Marchetti M. On the effectiveness of machine and deep learning for cyber security. In: 10th International Conference on Cyber Conflict (CyCon). Tallinn, Estonia; 2018

[24] Hatcher WG, Yu W. A survey of deep learning: Platforms, applications and emerging research trends. Human-Centered Smart Systems and Technologies. 2018;**6**:24411-24432

[25] E. A. The Theano Development. Theano: A Python framework for fast computation of mathematical expressions. In: arXiv preprint arXi; 2016

[26] The Microsoft Cognitive Toolkit. 2017. Available from: https://docs.microsoft.com/en-us/cognitive-toolkit/

[27] Shi S, Wang Q, Xu P, Chu X. Benchmarking state-of-the-art deep learning software tools. In: 7th International Conference on Cloud Computing and Big Data (CCBD). Macau, China; 2017

[28] Keras: The Python Deep Learning Library. 2017. Available from: https://keras.io/

[29] Torch: A Scientific Computing Framework for LuaJIT. 2017. Available from: http://torch.ch/

[30] Giang N, Dlugolinsky S, Bobák M, Tran V, García L, Heredia I, et al. Machine learning and deep learning frameworks and libraries for large-scale data mining. Artificial Intelligence Review. 2019;**52**(1):77-124

[31] Maryam NM, Villanustre F, Khoshgoftaar TM, Seliya N, Wald R, Muharemagic E. Deep learning applications and challenges in big data analytics. Journal of Big Data. 2015;**2**(1):1

[32] Yann L, Bottou L, Bengio Y, Haffner P. Gradient-based learning applied to document recognition. Proceedings of the IEEE. 1998;**86**(11):2278-2324

[33] Ian G, Bengio Y, Courville A. Deep learning. In: Adaptive Computation And Machine Learning, Cambridge. Cambridge USA: MIT Press; 2016

[34] Mahmood A, Shrestha A. Review of deep learning algorithms and architectures. IEEE Access. 2019;7:53040-53065

[35] Kumar OS, Joshi N. Rule power factor a new interest measure in associative classification. Procedia Computer Science. 2016;**93**:12-18

[36] Sharma O, Kumar S, Joshi N. Significant rule power an algorithm for new interest measure. In: Smart Computing and Informatics. Singapore: Smart Innovation, Systems and Technologies; 2018

[37] Dong C, Loy CC, He K, Tang X. Learning a deep convolutional network for image super-resolution. In: European Conference on Computer Vision. Cham; 2014

[38] Seonwoo M, Lee B, Yoon S. Deep learning in bioinformatics. Briefings in Bioinformatics. 2017;**18**(5):851-869

[39] Pathmind. 2019. Available from: https://pathmind.com/wiki/open-datasets

Chapter 2

Advances in Convolutional Neural Networks

Wen Xu, Jing He, Yanfeng Shu and Hui Zheng

Abstract

Deep Learning, also known as deep representation learning, has dramatically improved the performances on a variety of learning tasks and achieved tremendous successes in the past few years. Specifically, artificial neural networks are mainly studied, which mainly include Multilayer Perceptrons (MLPs), Convolutional Neural Networks (CNNs) and Recurrent Neural Networks (RNNs). Among these networks, CNNs got the most attention due to the kernel methods with the weight sharing mechanism, and achieved state-of-the-art in many domains, especially computer vision. In this research, we conduct a comprehensive survey related to the recent improvements in CNNs, and we demonstrate these advances from the low level to the high level, including the convolution operations, convolutional layers, architecture design, loss functions, and advanced applications.

Keywords: deep learning, CNNs, kernel methods, weight sharing, comprehensive survey

1. Introduction

Convolutional Neural Networks (CNNs) are specially designed to handle data that consists of multiple arrays/matrixes such as an image composed of three matrixes in RGB channels [1]. The key idea behind CNNs is the convolution operation, which is to use multiple small kernels/filters to extract local features by sliding over the same input. Each kernel can output a feature map and all the feature maps are concatenated together, this is also known as a convolutional layer and it is the core component in a CNN. Note that these concatenated maps can be further processed by the next layer. To reduce the computational cost, the pooling operation such as maximum pooling is usually applied on these feature maps. A typical CNN is usually structured as a series of layers, including multiple convolutional layers and a few of fully connected layers. For example, the famous LeNet [2] consists of two convolutional layers and three fully connected layers, and the pooling operation is used after each convolutional layer.

In addition to building a neural network, a loss function is essential to measure the model performance. Therefore, the process of training a CNN model is transformed into an optimization problem, which normally seeks to minimize the value of the loss function over the training data. Specifically, a gradient-descent based algorithm is usually adopted to iteratively optimize the parameters in a CNN.

Figure 1 shows the high-level abstraction of CNNs in this survey. Specifically, we firstly introduce two types of convolution operations in Section 2. Then four

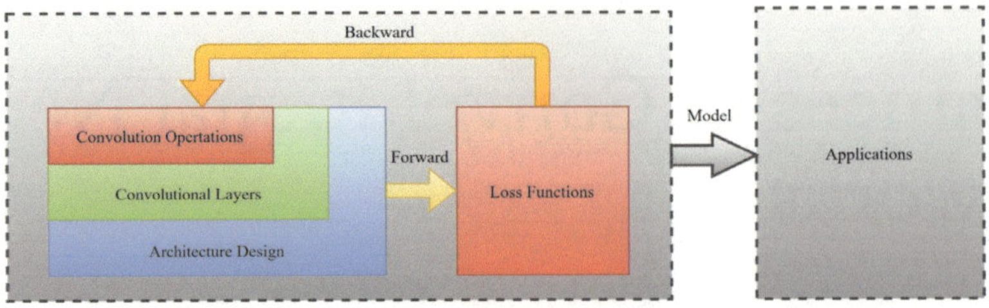

Figure 1.
High-level abstraction of convolutional neural networks in this survey.

methods are summarized for constructing convolutional layers in CNNs in Section 3. In Section 4, we group the current CNN architectures into three types: encoder, encoder-decoder and GANs. Next, we discuss two main types of loss functions in Section 5. In Section 6, we give the advanced applications based on the three types of CNN structures. Finally in Section 7, we conclude this research and give future trends.

2. Convolution operations

The main reason why CNNs are so successful on a variety of problems is that kernels (also known as filters) with fixed numbers of parameters are adopted to handle spacial data such as images. In particular the weight sharing mechanism can help reduce the number of parameters for low computational cost while remaining the spacial invariance properties. In general, there are mainly two types of convolution operations, including basic convolution and transposed convolution.

2.1 Basic convolution and dilated kernels

As shown on the left in **Figure 2**, convolution operation essentially is a linear model for the local spacial input. Specifically, it only performs the sum of element-wise dot products between the local input and the kernels (usually including a bias), and output a value after an activation function. Each kernel slides overall spacial locations in the input with a fixed step. The result is that we can get an 1-channel feature map. Note that there are generally many kernels in one convolutional layer, and all of the output feature maps are concatenated together, e.g., if the number of kernels used in this convolutional layer is D_O, we can get an $O \in \mathcal{R}^{3\times3\times D_O}$ feature map.

While the kernel size of 3×3 is widely used in current CNNs, we may need large receptive fields in the input for observing more information during each convolution operation. However, if we directly increase the size of kernels such as

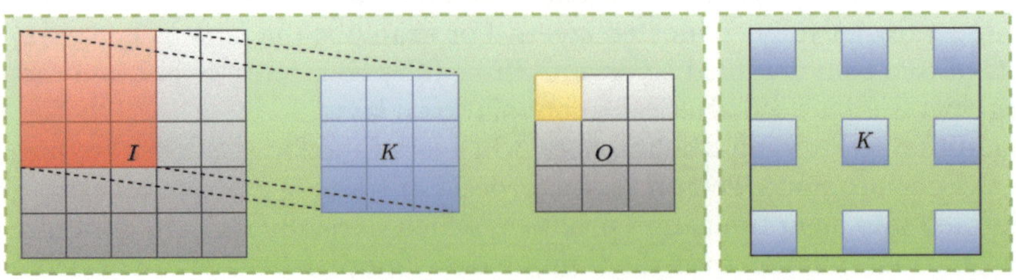

Figure 2.
Left: *A demonstration of basic 2D convolution with a* $3 \times 3 \times D_I$ *kernel (stride = 1, padding = 0),* $I \in \mathcal{R}^{5\times5\times D_I}$ *is the spacial input and* $O \in \mathcal{R}^{3\times3}$ *is the 1-channel output feature map.* ***Right:*** *A dilated kernel for increasing the receptive fields in the input, where the empty space between each element represents 0.*

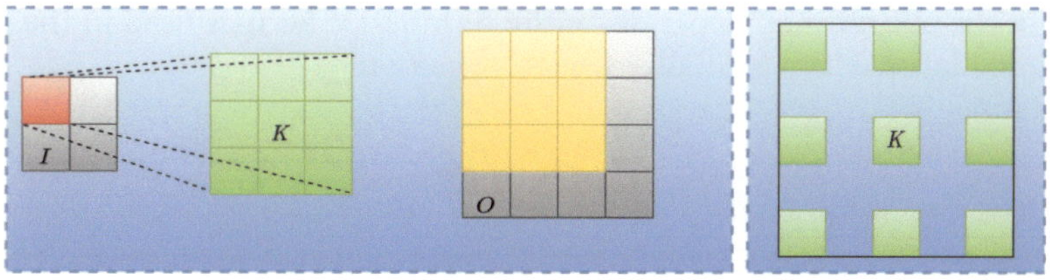

Figure 3.
Left: *A demonstration of transposed 2D convolution with a* $3 \times 3 \times D_I$ *kernel (stride = 1, padding = 0),* $I \in \mathcal{R}^{2\times2\times D_I}$ *is the spacial input and* $O \in \mathcal{R}^{4\times4}$ *is the 1-channel output feature map. Note that the receptive fields in O can overlap and we normally sum the values where output overlaps.* ***Right:*** *A dilated kernel for increasing the receptive fields in the input, where the empty space between each element represents 0.*

$K = 9 \times 9 \times D_I$, where D_I is the depth of input, the total number of parameters will increase dramatically and the computational cost will be prohibitive. In practical, as shown on the right in **Figure 2**, we can insert zeros between each element in the kernels and get dilated kernels. For example, dilated kernels have been applied in many tasks such as image segmentation [3], translation tasks [4] and speech recognition [5].

2.2 Transposed convolution and dilated kernels

Normally the size of output feature maps generated from the basic convolution is smaller than the input space (i.e., the dimension of input I is $5 \times 5 \times D_I$ and the dimension of output O is 3×3 in **Figure 2**), which results in high-level abstraction by using multiple convolutional layers. Transposed convolution can be seen as a reverse idea from basic convolution. Its primary purpose is to obtain an output feature map that is bigger than the input space. As shown on the left in **Figure 3**, the size of the input I is $2 \times 2 \times D_I$, after transposed convolution, we can have a 4×4 feature map O. Specifically, during transposed convolution, each output filed in O is just the kernel multiplied by the scalar value of one element in I.

Similarly, we can still use dilated kernels in transposed convolution. The main reason why we need transposed convolution is that it is the fundamental idea to construct a decoder network, which is used to map a latent space into an output image, such as the decoders in U-Net [6] and GANs. Specifically, the transposed convolution is widely used in tasks such as model visualization [7], image segmentation [6], image classification [8] and image super-resolution [9].

3. Convolutional layers

The core components in CNNs are convolutional layers. In the last section, we have demonstrated two types of convolution operations and they are the main idea to construct convolutional layers. In this part, we summarize the main methods in deep learning for building convolutional layers, including basic convolutional layers, convolutional layers with shortcut connection, convolutional layers with mixed kernels and convolutional capsule layers.

3.1 Basic convolutional layers

Recall that there are normally D_O kernels in one convolutional layer, where D_O also denotes the depth of the output feature map. In other words, the number of channels in the output map depends on the number of kernels used in the convolutional layer. More formally, we can denote it as

$$O = \sum_{i=1}^{D_O} I * K_i \tag{1}$$

where $*$ represents the convolution operation which has been addressed above, $\sum$ denotes the concatenation operation and $O \in \mathcal{R}^{W_O H_O D_O}$ is the output feature map. After convolution operation, a no-linear activation function is applied on each element in the concatenated feature map, which can be denoted as

$$O = \sigma(O) \tag{2}$$

While there are many variants related to the activation function, the typical ones which are widely adopted are ReLU $\sigma(x) = \max(0, x)$, tanh $\sigma(x) = \frac{e^x - e^{-x}}{e^x + e^{-x}}$ and sigmoid $\sigma(x) = \frac{1}{1+e^{-x}}$. Note that the non-linear activation functions are essential for building multi-layer networks, as it shows that a two-layer network with enough neurons can uniformly approximate any functions, which is also known as universal approximation theorem [10].

Note that after convolution operation, the width and height of the output feature map $O \in \mathcal{R}^{W_O H_O D_O}$ are usually close to the width and height of the input $I \in \mathcal{R}^{W_I H_I D_I}$. To further reduce the dimensions of the output feature maps for reducing computational cost, the pooling operation is widely used in the current CNNs. Specifically, for 2D pooling operation, two main hyper-parameters are involved: the filter size $F \times F$ and stride S. And after pooling operation, the width of the feature map O is reduced to $W_O = (W_O - F)/S + 1$ and the height of the feature map O is $H_O = (H_O - F)/S + 1$. In brief, we can have

$$O = pool(O) \tag{3}$$

where $pool()$ denotes the pooling operation discussed above. Typical pooling operations includes max-pooling and average-pooling. A general choice to conduct pooling operation is to use $stride = 2$ with 2×2 filter, which means that each 4 pixels in the 2D feature map O will be compressed into 1 pixel. Using a toy example, suppose that there are only four pixels $O = \begin{bmatrix} 1 & 2 \\ 3 & 4 \end{bmatrix}$, then $pool_{max}(O) = [4]$ or $pool_{avg}(O) = [2.5]$.

3.2 Convolutional layers with shortcut connection

It is true that deep neural networks normally can learn better representation from the data than shallow neural networks. However, stacking more layers in a CNN can lead to the problems of vanishing or exploding gradients, which make the networks hard to optimize. A simple and effective way to address this problem is to use shortcut connections, which can help directly transform the information from the previous layer to the current layer in a network.

$$O = \sigma\left(\left(\sum_{i=1}^{D_O} I_{current} * K_i\right) \oplus I_{previous}\right) \tag{4}$$

Note that $\oplus$ can denote two types of operations.

- **Element-Wise Sum:** Each element in $I_{current}$ is added by the corresponding element in $I_{previous}$, which means that the dimensions of $I_{current}$ and $I_{previous}$ must be the same, and the result is that we can get an output O of the same size. This type of operation is well known as **identity shortcut connection** and it is the core idea in ResNet [11, 12]. The main advantage is that it does not add any extra parameters or computational complexity. The disadvantage is due to its inflexible.

- **Concatenation:** We can concatenate the current output and previous input together. Suppose the size of the current output feature map is WHD_O and the size of the previous input is WHD_I, after concatenation, we can have a concatenated feature map O with a size of $WH(D_O + D_I)$. Note that the widths and heights of input and output must be the same. The advantage is that we can remain the information from the previous layers. The disadvantage is that we have to use extra parameters to handle the concatenated feature map O. (i.e., the depth of kernels for processing feature map O is $(D_O + D_I)$.) Specifically, this type of convolutional layers is broadly adopted in networks for image segmentation such as U-Net [6].

3.3 Convolutional layers with mixed kernels

So far we have demonstrated that we normally use many convolutional kernels with the same size in one convolutional layer such as 3×3. To enlarge the receptive field, we may adopt the dilated kernels instead. However, it is difficult to know what size of kernels we should use in a CNN. Naturally, we may apply different sizes of kernels in each convolutional layer. E.g., both 1×1, 3×3 and 5×5 kernels are adopted in one convolutional layer. More formally, we define one convolutional layer with mixed kernels as

$$O = \sigma\left(\sum_{i=1}^{D_O^1} I * K_i^{1\times1} + \sum_{i=1}^{D_O^2} I * K_i^{3\times3} + \sum_{i=1}^{D_O^3} I * K_i^{5\times5} + pool(I)\right) \tag{5}$$

where pool(I) denotes the pooling operation such as max-pooling. Therefore, the size of the output feature map is $W_O H_O (D_O^1 + D_O^2 + D_O^3 + D_I)$.

However, if we directly add different sizes of kernels in one convolutional layer, the computational cost involved will increase sharply. In the inception module [13, 14], a 1×1 convolutional layer is applied before 3×3 and 5×5 convolutional layers in order to reduce the convolutional cost.

3.4 Convolutional capsule layers

> *"The pooling operation used in convolutional neural networks is a big mistake and the fact that it works so well is a disaster."—Geoffrey Hinton.*

In general, pooling operation is essential to reduce the size of output feature maps so that we can obtain high-level abstractions from input by stacking multiple convolutional layers in a CNN. However, the cost is that some information in the feature maps has been abandoned such as conducting max-pooling.

In 2017 [15], Hinton et al. proposed an alluring version of convolutional architectures, which is known as capsule networks, followed by the updated versions in 2018 [16] and 2019 [17]. The convolutional capsule layers in capsule networks are very similar to the traditional convolutional layers. The main difference is that each capsule (i.e., an element in convolutional feature maps) has a weight matrix W_{ij} (i.e., the sizes are 8×16 in [15] and 4×4 in [16] respectively).

4. Architecture design

Although numerous variants of CNN architectures for solving different tasks are proposed from the deep learning community every year, their essential components and over-all structures are very similar. We group the recent classic network structures into three main types, including encoder, encoder-decoder and GANs.

4.1 Encoder

In 1990, LeCun et al. proposed a seminal network called LeNet [2], which help establish the modern CNN structure. Since then, many new methods and compositions are proposed to handle the difficulties encountered in training deep networks for challenging tasks such as objective detection and recognition in computer vision. Some representative works in recent years are AlexNet [18], ZFNet [7], VGGNet [19], GoogleNet [13], ResNet [11], Inception [14]. As mentioned earlier, new methods for constructing convolutional layers in these networks are proposed, e.g., shortcut connection [11] and mixed kernels [14, 20].

In general, the above-mentioned networks can all be regarded as encoders, in which each input such as an image is encoded into a high-level feature representation, as shown on the left in **Figure 4**. And this encoded representation can be further used for, such as image classification, object detection etc. In some literatures, an encoder is also called as a feature extractor. Specifically, the basic convolutional layers are the main components for constructing an encoder network, by stacking multiple layers, each layer in the network can learn high-level abstractions from previous layers [1]. More formally, an encoder network can be written as

$$Z = \mathcal{F}_{encoder}(X; \Theta) \tag{6}$$

where X is the input, Θ is the parameters to learn (e.g., kernels and bias) in the network and Z denotes the encoded representation such as a vector.

4.2 Encoder-decoder

In some specific tasks such as image segmentation [20], our goal is to map an input image to a segmented output image rather than an abstraction. An encoder-decoder structure is specifically designed for solving this type of task. There are

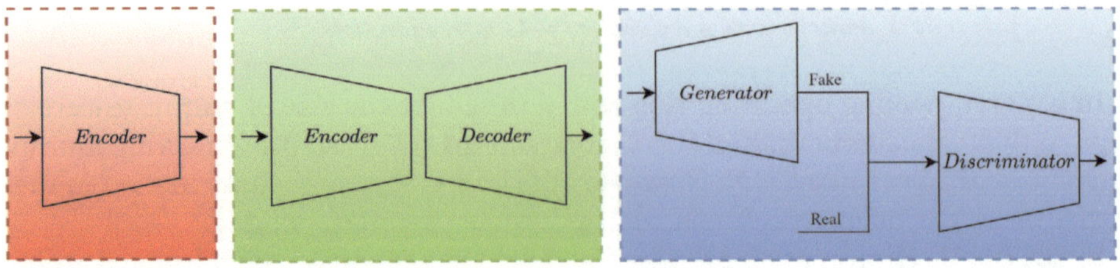

Figure 4.
Left: *An encoder network.* ***Middle:*** *An encoder-decoder network.* ***Right:*** *Generative adversarial networks.*

many possible ways to implement an encoder-decoder structure, and many variants have also been proposed to improve the drawbacks in the last few years. A naive version of encoder-decoder network which was introduced in [20] can be denoted as

$$Z = \mathcal{F}_{encoder}(X; \theta_{encoder}) \tag{7}$$

$$\hat{X} = \mathcal{F}_{decoder}(Z; \theta_{decoder}) \tag{8}$$

where $\mathcal{F}_{encoder}$ denotes an encoder CNN to map an input sample to a representation Z and $\mathcal{F}_{decoder}$ represents a decoder CNN to reconstruct the input sample with Z. Specifically, CNN encoders usually conducts basic convolution operations (i.e., Section 2.1) and CNN decoders perform transposed convolution operations (i.e., Section 2.2).

As shown in the middle in **Figure 4**, an encoder-decoder network is still one complete network and we can train it with an end-to-end method. Note that there are generally many convolutional layers in each coder network, which results that it can be challenging to train a deep encoder-decoder network directly. Recall that the shortcut connection is often adopted to address the problems in deep CNNs. Naturally, we can add connections between the encoder and the decoder. An influential network based on this idea is U-Net [6], which is widely applied in many challenging domains such as medical image segmentation. The above two equations can also be rewritten as a composition of two functions.

$$\hat{X} = \mathcal{F}_{decoder} \circ \mathcal{F}_{encoder}(X; \Theta) = \mathcal{F}_{autoencoder}(X; \Theta) \tag{9}$$

Specifically, in unsupervised learning, an encoder-decoder network is also well known as autoencoder. And there are many variants of autoencoders proposed in recent years, some famous ones including variational autoencoder [21], denoising variational autoencoder [22] and conditional variational autoencoder [23, 24].

4.3 GANs

Since generative adversarial networks were firstly proposed by Goodfellow et al. [25] in 2014, this type of architectures for playing two-player minimax game has been most extensively studied. Partly because it is an unsupervised learning method and we can obtain a fancy generator network which can help generate fake examples from a latent space (i.e., a vector with some random noise). On the right in **Figure 4** shows the basic structure of GANs, in which a generator network can map some input noise into a fake example and make it look as real as possible and a discriminator network always tries to identify the fake sample from its input. By iteratively training the two players, they can both improve their methods. More formally, we can have

$$\hat{Y} = \mathcal{D}(\mathcal{G}(L; \theta_{\mathcal{G}}), X_{real}, \theta_{\mathcal{D}}) \tag{10}$$

where $\mathcal{G}$ denotes the generator function and $\mathcal{D}$ represents the discriminator function. L is the latent space input in the generator, and its output is a fake example. X_{real} is the real samples we have collected. And $\hat{Y} \in [0, 1]$ is the predicted result of the discriminator to show whether the input is real or fake.

As shown in **Table 1**, numerous variants of GANs architectures can be found in the recently published literatures and we broadly summarize these representative networks according to their published time. Note that the fundamental methods behind these architectures are very similar.

Name	Year	Summary
GANs [25]	2014	The original version of GANs, where $\mathcal{G}$ and $\mathcal{D}$ are implemented with fully connected neural networks.
Conditional GANs [26]	2014	Labels are included in $\mathcal{G}$ and $\mathcal{D}$.
Laplacian Pyramid GANs [27]	2015	CNNs with the laplacian pyramid method.
Deep Convolutional GANs [28]	2015	Transposed convolutional layers are used to construct $\mathcal{G}$.
Bidirectional GANs [29]	2016	An extra encoder was adopted based on the traditional GANs.
Semi-supervised GANs [30]	2016	The $\mathcal{D}$ can also classify the real samples while distinguishing the real and fake.
InfoGANs [31]	2016	An extra classifier was added into the GANs.
Energy-based GANs [32]	2016	The $\mathcal{D}$ was replaced with an encoder-decoder network.
Auxiliary Classifier GANs [33]	2017	An auxiliary classifier was used in the $\mathcal{D}$.
Progressive GANs [34]	2017	Progressive steps are adopted to explain the networks.
BigGANs [35]	2018	A large GANs with self-attention module and hinge loss.
Self-attention GANs [36]	2019	The self-attention mechanism is proposed to build $\mathcal{G}$ and $\mathcal{D}$.
Label-noise Robust GANs [37]	2019	A noise transition model is included in $\mathcal{D}$.
AutoGANs [38]	2019	The neural architecture search algorithm is used to obtain $\mathcal{G}$ and $\mathcal{D}$.
Your Local GANs [39]	2020	A new local sparse attention layer was proposed.
MSG-GANs [40]	2020	There are connections from $\mathcal{G}$ to $\mathcal{D}$.

Table 1.
Representative architectures of GANs in recent years.

5. Loss functions

Before introducing the loss functions, we need to understand that the ultimate goal to train a neural network $\mathcal{F}(X;\Theta)$ is to find a suitable set of parameters Θ so that our model can achieve good performance on the unseen samples (i.e., test dataset). The typical way to search Θ in machine learning is to use loss functions as a criterion during training. In other words, training neural networks is equivalent to optimizing the loss functions by back-propagation. Accurately, a loss function outputs a scalar value which is regarded as a criterion for measuring the difference between the predicted result and the true label over one sample. And during training, our goal is to minimize the scalar value over m training samples (i.e., cost function). Therefore, as shown in **Figure 1**, loss functions play a significant role in constructing CNNs.

$$\mathcal{J} = \frac{1}{m}\sum_{i=1}^{m} \mathcal{L}_i \tag{11}$$

where $\mathcal{L}_i$ denotes a loss function for the training sample i, and $\mathcal{J}$ is often known as cost function, which is just the mean of the sum of the losses over m training samples (i.e., usually a batch of m training samples is fed into a CNN during each iteration of training).

Note that there are numerous variants of loss functions used in the deep learning literature. However, the fundamental theories behind them are very similar. We group them into two categories, namely Divergence Loss Functions and Margin Loss Functions. And we also introduce six typical and classic loss functions that are commonly used for training neural networks.

5.1 Divergence loss functions

Divergence loss functions denote a family of loss functions based on computing the divergences between the predicted results and true labels, mainly including Kullback-Leibler Divergence, Log Loss, Mean Squared Error.

5.1.1 Kullback-Leibler divergence

Before introducing the Kullback–Leibler divergence, we need to understand that the fundamental goal of deep learning is to learn a data distribution Q over the training dataset so that Q is close to the true data distribution P. Back in 1951, Kullback-Leibler divergence was proposed to measure the difference between two distributions on the same probability space [41]. It is defined as

$$\begin{aligned} D_{KL}(P\|Q) &= \sum_X P(X) log P(X) - \sum_X P(X) log Q(X) \\ &= \sum_X P(X)\, log\, \frac{P(X)}{Q(X)} \end{aligned} \tag{12}$$

where $D_{KL}(P\|Q)$ denotes the Kullback–Leibler divergence from Q to P. $\sum_X P(X) log P(X)$ is the entropy of P and $\sum_X P(X) log Q(X)$ is the cross entropy of P and Q. There is also a symmetrized form of the Kullback–Leibler divergence, which is known as the Jensen–Shannon divergence. It is a measure of the similarity between P and Q.

$$JSD(P\|Q) = \frac{1}{2} D_{KL}\left(P\| \frac{P+Q}{2}\right) + \frac{1}{2} D_{KL}\left(Q\| \frac{P+Q}{2}\right) \tag{13}$$

Specifically, $JSD(P\|Q) = 0$ means the two distributions are the same. Therefore, if we minimize the Jensen-Shannon divergence, we can make the distribution Q close to the distribution P. More Specifically, if Q denotes the distribution on data, and P represents the distribution which is learned by a CNN model. By minimizing the divergence, we can learn a model which is close to the true data distribution. This is the main idea of GANs. The loss function of GANs is defined as

$$\min_{\mathcal{G}} \max_{\mathcal{D}} : \quad \mathbb{E}_{X\sim P(X)}\, log\, \mathcal{D}(X; \Theta_{\mathcal{D}}) + \mathbb{E}_{L\sim Q(L)}\, log\, (1 - \mathcal{D}(\mathcal{G}(L; \Theta_{\mathcal{G}}); \Theta_{\mathcal{D}})) \tag{14}$$

where $\mathcal{G}$ denotes the generator and $\mathcal{D}$ denotes the discriminator. And our goal is to try to make $Q(\mathcal{G}(L))$ close to $P(X)$. In other words, when the generative distribution of fake examples is close to the distribution of real samples, the discriminator cannot distinguish between the fake and the real.

5.1.2 Log loss

Log loss is widely used in the current deep neural networks due to its simplicity and power. The binary log loss function is defined as

$$\mathcal{L}_{binary} = -Ylog(\hat{Y}) - (1 - Y)\, log\, (1 - \hat{Y}) \quad (Y \in [0, 1]) \tag{15}$$

where $Y \in [0, 1]$ denotes the binary label for a sample and $\hat{Y}$ is the predicted result, (i.e., given a training sample with its corresponding label $\{X, Y\}$, we can have an output predicted result with an encoder network $\hat{Y} = \mathcal{F}_{encoder}(X, \Theta)$.)

When the learning task is multi-class classification, each sample label is normally encoded with the one-hot-encoding format, which can be denoted as $Y = [y_1, y_2, \dots, y_{nclass}]^T$, i.e., if the label is 3, then only $y_3 = 1$ and the others are all given the value of 0. Therefore, the log loss for one sample can be written as

$$\mathcal{L}_{log} = -\sum_{i=1}^{nclass} 1\{y_i = 1\}\, log\, (\hat{y}_i) \tag{16}$$

where $\hat{y}_i$ is the predicted result for the true label y_i. $1\{y_i = 1\}$ denotes the indicator function, which means that its output is 1 if $y_i = 1$, otherwise it outputs 0.

We may wonder why the log loss is a reasonable choice. Informally, let Y denotes the data distribution and $\hat{Y}$ denotes the distribution leaned by our model, then based on Kullback–Leibler divergence, we can have

$$D_{KL}(Y \| \hat{Y}) = \sum YlogY - \sum Ylog\hat{Y} \tag{17}$$

And our goal is to minimize the divergence between Y and $\hat{Y}$ so that the distribution obtained by our model is close to the true data distribution. Because the term $\sum YlogY$ is the entropy related to data, and we only need to optimize the cross entropy term $-\sum Ylog\hat{Y}$. Therefore, log loss is also well known as cross-entropy loss.

5.1.3 Mean squared error

Probably the mean squared error is one of the most familiar loss functions as it is really like the least square loss function. It directly calculates the difference between the predicted result and the true label, which is denoted as

$$\mathcal{L}_{mean} = -\frac{1}{2}(Y - \hat{Y})^2 \tag{18}$$

One example which can help us deeply understand the mean squared error is that minimize the mean squared loss of a linear regression model is equivalent to maximum likelihood. In other words, this is a method to optimize the parameters of our model so that the distribution learned by our model is most probable under the observed training data. Therefore, the fundamental goal is still the same as above, which is to make the model distribution and the data distribution as close as possible.

5.2 Margin loss functions

Margin loss functions represent a family of margin maximizing loss functions. The typical functions include Hinge Loss, Contrastive Loss and Triplet Loss. Unlike the divergence loss functions, margin loss functions calculate the relative distances between outputs and they are more flexible in terms of training data.

5.2.1 Hinge loss

Hinge loss is well known to train Support Vector Machine classifiers. Specifically, there are two main types of hinge losses. The first type is for each sample with only one correct label, it is denoted as

$$\mathcal{L}_{hinge} = \sum_{i \neq k}^{nclass} \max\left(0, \Delta + \hat{y}_i - \hat{y}_k\right)^p \quad \left(y_k = 1, \sum_{i \neq k}^{nclass} y_i = 0\right) \tag{19}$$

where y_i denotes each element in the one-hot-encoding label, y_k is the correct class. $\hat{y}_i$ represents the predicted result of our neural network for each class. $\Delta = 1$ is the standard choice for the margin. If $p = 1$, the above loss denotes the standard Hinge loss, and if $p = 2$, it is the Squared Hinge loss.

However, in real tasks such as attribute classification, each samples can have multiple correct labels. e.g., a photo posted on Facebook may include a set of hashtags. Therefore, the second type for multiple labels is

$$\mathcal{L}_{hinge} = \sum_{i=1}^{nclass} \max\left(0, \Delta - \delta(y_i = 1)\hat{y}_i\right)^p \tag{20}$$

where $\delta(y_i = 1) = +1$ if $y_i = 1$, otherwise $\delta(y_i = 1) = -1$. $\Delta = 1$ is still the common choice for the margin and $p = 1$ or $p = 2$.

5.2.2 Contrastive loss

Contrastive loss is specially designed for measuring the similarity of a pair of training samples. Considering two pairs of samples $\{X_a, X_p\}$ and $\{X_a, X_n\}$, where X_a is known as an anchor sample and X_p denotes the positive sample and X_n represents the negative sample, Specifically, if the pair $\{X_a, X_p\}$ is matching, then the loss for the pair is the distance between their outputs from the network $d(Z_a, Z_p)$. While if the pair $\{X_a, X_n\}$ is not matching and the distance of their outputs from the model is small than the pre-defined margin $(0, \Delta - d(Z_a, Z_n)) > 0$, then we need also to calculate the loss. Formally, we can have

$$\mathcal{L}_{contrastive} = \begin{cases} d(Z_a, Z_p) & \text{if matched pair} \\ \max\left(0, \Delta - d(Z_a, Z_n)\right) & \text{if unmatched pair} \end{cases} \tag{21}$$

where d can be the Euclidean distance, (i.e., $d(Z_a, Z_p)) = \|Z_a - Z_n\|_2)$. Alternatively, the above equation can be rewritten as

$$\mathcal{L}_{contrastive} = yd(Z_a, Z_p) + (1 - y)\max\left(0, \Delta - d(Z_a, Z_n)\right) \tag{22}$$

where $y = 1$ if the given pair is matching, otherwise $y = 0$. Δ is the margin which can affect the loss calculating for the unmatched pairs.

5.2.3 Triplet loss

Triplet loss looks similar to the contrastive loss, but it is a measure of the difference between the matched pair and the unmatched pair. Considering three samples $\{X_a, X_p, X_n\}$, the Triplet loss is denoted as

$$\mathcal{L}_{triplet} = \max\left(0, \Delta + d(Z_a, Z_p) - d(Z_a, Z_n)\right) \tag{23}$$

Note that minimize the loss function is equivalent to minimizing the distances of matched pairs and maximizing the distances of unmatched pairs.

6. Advanced applications

One of the most exciting areas in deep learning is that we can apply neural networks to a numerous number of applications that cannot be solved well or be handled by the traditional machine learning method. In this section, we summarize the typical advances that CNNs has achieved based on the three types of CNN structures.

6.1 Applications with encoders

6.1.1 Image classification

A basic task in machine learning is classification, which is the problem of identifying to which of a list of labels a new sample belongs, such as the well-known CIFAR-10 dataset, in which there are 10 categories of images and the goal is to train a model for correctly classifying an unseen image based on observing the training dataset. In particular, CNNs have made many breakthroughs on large scale image datasets such as the ImageNet challenge [18]. As mentioned in Section 4.1, the classic encoders such as AlexNet [18], ZFNet [7], VGGNet [19], GoogleNet [13], ResNet [11], Inception [14] are regarded as the milestones in the past few years. The successes of these encoders are all based on supervised learning, which means that manual labelling is essential for the dataset such as the ImageNet dataset [42]. Specifically, a labeled dataset is normally divided into training and test dataset (may also include a validation dataset), and our goal is to achieve good performance on the test dataset after training a neural network with the training dataset, and the pre-trained model can be further used for classifying new images that are from the same data distribution space.

Classification can also be treated as a fundamental problem in machine learning, the successes of these encoders on image classification also help establish the foundation for many other applications. Specifically, we can utilize an encoder to extract high-level representation from the low-level input image, and the obtained representation can be further used for many other applications.

6.1.2 Object detection

In addition to image classification, object detection is also very important in computer vision. Image classification gives us the answer to what a given image is, and object detection is about telling us the specific positions of objects in an image. Specifically, the goal is to train an encoder to output a suitable bounding box and associated class probabilities for each object in a given image. Two typical methods are widely used in the current computer vision, including YOLO [43] and SSD [44]. The core idea of YOLO is that object detection is treated as an regression problem, which means that each image is divided into multiple grids and each grid cell outputs a pre-defined number of bounding boxes, the corresponding confidence for each box and class probabilities [43]. Since the first version of YOLO was proposed, the updated versions have also been proposed. SSD is a more simple method, which utilizes a set of default boxes with different aspect ratios, and each box outputs the shape offsets and the class confidences [44].

6.1.3 Pose estimation

The multiple levels of representations learned in the multiple layers of CNNs can also be used for solving the task of human-body pose estimation. Specifically, there are mainly two types of approaches, including regression of body joint coordinates and heat-map for each body part. In 2014, a framework called DeepPose [45] was introduced to learn pose estimation by a deep CNN, in which estimating human-body pose is equivalent to regressing the body joint coordinates. There are also some extension works based on this method, such as a process called iterative error feedback [46], which encompasses both the input and output spaces of CNN for enhancing the performance. In 2014, Tompson et al. [47] propose a hybrid architecture which consists of a CNN and a Markov Random Field, in particular the output of the CNN for an input image is a heat-map. Some recent works based on the heat-map method such as [48], in which a multi-context attention mechanism was proposed to incorporate with CNNs.

6.2 Applications with encoder-decoders

6.2.1 Image restoration

The operation of image restoration is to recover a damaged or corrupt image for the clean image such as image denoising and super-resolution. Therefore, a natural way to implement this idea is to utilize a pre-trained encoder-decoder network, where the encoder can map a noise image into a high-level representation, and the decoder can transform the representation into an original image. For example, Mao et al. [49] apply a deep convolutional encoder-decoder network for image restoration, in particular the shortcut connection method is adopted between the encoder and decoder, which has been demonstrated in Section 3.2. And the transposed convolution is used for constructing the decoder network, as mentioned in Section 2.2. Similar work in [50] has also been introduced for image restoration, in which a residual method is used in the network (i.e., in Section 3.2).

6.2.2 Image segmentation

The task of image segmentation is to map an input image into a segmented output image. The encoder-decoder networks have been developed dramatically in recent years and achieve a significant impact on computer vision. Specifically, there are mainly two types of tasks including semantic segmentation and instance segmentation. In 2015, Long et al. [20] firstly showed that an end-to-end fully CNN can achieve state-of-art in image segmentation tasks. Similar work has also been introduced in [6] in 2015, in which a U-Net architecture is proposed for medical image segmentation, and the main advance in this architecture is that the shortcut connection method is also used between the encoder and decoder network. Since then, a series of papers based on these two methods have been published. In particular nowadays the U-Net based architectures are widely used for the medical image diagnosis.

6.2.3 Image captioning

One of the exciting applications achieved by CNNs is image captioning, which is to describe the content of an input image with natural language. The basic idea is as follows: Firstly, a pre-trained CNN encoder is used to extract some high-level features from an input image. Secondly, these features are typically fed into an recurrent neural network for generating a sentence. For example, Li et al. [51] proposed a fully convolutional localization network for extracting representation from images and the decoder for generating captions is LSTM. Recently, attention mechanism has been widely used for sequence processing and achieved significant improvements such as machine translation, Huang et al. [52] introduce an encoder-decoder framework, where an attention module is used in the encoder and decoder respectively. Specifically, the encoder is a CNN based network.

6.2.4 Speech processing

Note that speech signals exhibit spectral variations and correlations, CNNs are very suitable to reduce them. Therefore, CNNs can also be utilized for the task of speech processing, such as speech recognition. Sainath1 et al. [53] applied deep CNNs for large vocabulary speech tasks. In [54–56], the CNNs are used for speech recognition. And the fundamental methods are very similar, both of them use the CNNs to extract features from the raw input, and then these features are fed into an decoder for the specific learning tasks.

6.3 Applications with GANs

6.3.1 Image generation

The most typical application of GANs is to generate fake examples. Recall that there normally are two dependent networks in GANs, including $\mathcal{G}$ and $\mathcal{D}$. Once the training process is finished, we can utilize $\mathcal{G}$ to generate fake samples from the training dataset.

Generating fake samples can be regarded as data augmentation, which means that these fake data can be further used to train models. Note that deep learning is also well known as a data-driven approach. In particular most of the advances that deep neural networks achieved are based on supervised learning. Specifically, the current successful neural network models usually consist of millions of parameters. And annotated data is essential to optimize these parameters for guaranteeing the model accuracy when conducting supervised learning. However, manually labeling data is time-consuming and expensive, especially in some specific domains such as medicine. Even more severe is that it can be hard to collect enough data due to the privacy concerns. There are numerous works to utilize GANs for enhancing model performance. E.g., in [57], a semi-supervised framework based on GANs is applied to semantic segmentation in order to address the lack of annotations. [58] is a work of utilizing synthetic medical images for enhancing the performance of liver lesion classification.

Despite the successes of GANs, generating high-resolution, diverse samples is still a challenging task. In [35], they introduce the progressive GANs which can generate high-resolution human faces. Another impressive work to generate realistic photographs is BigGANs [36].

6.3.2 Image translation

Another interesting application derived from GANs is image translation. While there are many specific applications, we summarize them into three categories, including translation of image to image, translation of text to image and translation of image to super-resolution.

Image to Image: The task of image-to-image translation is to learn a mapping $\mathcal{G}(X) \rightarrow Y$. E.g., Isola et al. [59] apply conditional GANs for an image-to-image task and achieve impressive results such as mapping sketches to photographs, black-white photographs to color etc. Another typical work is the CycleGANs [60], which can transfer a style of an image into another.

Text to Image: One of the interesting works from GANs is to synthesis a realistic image based on some text descriptions. E.g., "There is a little bird with red feather." Some representative works include: Reed et al. [61] introduce a text-conditional convolutional GANs. Zhang et al. [62] apply a StackGANs to synthesize high-quality images from text.

Super Resolution: The task of super-resolution is to map a low-resolution image to a high-resolution image. In 2017, ledig et al. [63] propose a framework named as SRGAN, which is regarded as the first work that has the ability to generate photo-realistic images for 4X upscaling factors. Specifically, the loss functions used in their framework consist of an adversarial loss and a content loss. In particular the content loss can help remain the original content from the input images.

6.3.3 Image editing

Image editing is regarded as a fundamental problem in computer vision. The emergence of GANs has also brought new chances for this task. In the past few years, GANs have been developed for image editing, such as image inpainting and image matting.

Image inpainting: The task of image inpainting is to recover an arbitrary damaged region in an image. Specifically, we can utilize the algorithm to learn the content and style of the image and generate the damaged part based on the input image, such as [64], in which they introduce a context encoder for natural image inpainting. And in [65, 66], their works mainly focus on human face completion.

Image matting: The goal of image matting is to separate the foreground object from the background in an image. This technique can be used for a wide range of applications such as photo editing and video post-production. And there are also some representative works such as [67, 68].

7. Summary and future trends

In this research, we have conducted a hierarchically-structured survey of the main components in CNNs from the low level to the high level, namely, convolution operations, convolutional layers, architecture design, loss functions. In addition to introducing the recent advances of these aspects in CNNs, we have also discussed the advanced applications based on the three types of architectures including encoder, encoder-decoder and GANs, from which we can see that CNNs have made numerous breakthroughs and achieved state-of-the-art in computer vision, natural language processing and speech recognition, especially these fantastic results based on GANs.

From the above analyses, we can summarize that the current development tendencies in CNNs mainly focus on designing new architectures and loss functions. Because these two aspects are the core parts when applying CNNs into various types of tasks. On the other hand, the fundamental ideas behind these various applications are very similar, as summarized above.

However, there are still many disadvantages in the current deep learning. The first problem is the requirement of large-scale datasets, in particular constructing a labeled dataset is very time-consuming and expensive such as in the medical domain. Therefore, we need to pay much more attention to semi-supervised learning and unsupervised learning. The second disadvantage is the high computational cost related to training deep CNNs, as the current standard CNN structures become deeper and deeper and they usually consists of millions of parameters. The third issue is that applying CNNs into tasks is not an easy job and it usually requires professional skills and experiences, because training a network involves a lot of hyper-parameters to tune, such as the number of kernels in each layer, the size of kernels, the total number of layers, learning rate etc.

Future work should focus on deep learning theory as the solid theory for supporting the current neural models is lacking. Unlike other machine learning algorithms such as support vector machines that have obvious mathematical logic, it is usually very hard to totally understand why a deep network can achieve such an excellent performance on a task. Therefore, based on the current developments of deep learning, we give three trends on which we need to work in the future: Neural Topologies such as the graph neural networks, Uncertainty Estimation such as Bayesian neural networks and Privacy Preservation.

Acknowledgements

This work is supported by China Scholarship Council and Data61 from CSIRO, Australia.

Conflict of interest

The authors declare no conflict of interest.

Author details

Wen Xu[1,2], Jing He[1*], Yanfeng Shu[2] and Hui Zheng[1]

1 Swinburne University of Technology, Australia

2 Data61, CSIRO, Australia

*Address all correspondence to: jinghe@swin.edu.au

References

[1] LeCun Y, Bengio Y, Hinton G. Deep learning. Nature. 2015;**521**(7553): 436-444

[2] LeCun Y, Boser BE, Denker JS, Henderson D, Howard RE, Hubbard WE, et al. Handwritten digit recognition with a back-propagation network. In: Advances in Neural Information Processing Systems. 1990. pp. 396-404

[3] Yu F, Koltun V. Multi-Scale Context Aggregation by Dilated Convolutions. arXiv preprint arXiv:1511.07122. November 23, 2015

[4] Kalchbrenner N, Espeholt L, Simonyan K, Oord AV, Graves A, Kavukcuoglu K. Neural Machine Translation in Linear Time. arXiv preprint arXiv:1610.10099. October 31, 2016

[5] Sercu T, Goel V. Dense prediction on sequences with time-dilated convolutions for speech recognition. arXiv preprint arXiv:1611.09288. November 28, 2016

[6] Ronneberger O, Fischer P, Brox T. U-net: Convolutional networks for biomedical image segmentation. In: International Conference on Medical Image Computing and Computer-Assisted Intervention. Cham: Springer; 2015. pp. 234-241

[7] Zeiler MD, Fergus R. Visualizing and understanding convolutional networks. In: European Conference on Computer Vision. Cham: Springer; 2014. pp. 818-833

[8] Zhang Y, Lee K, Lee H. Augmenting supervised neural networks with unsupervised objectives for large-scale image classification. In: International Conference on Machine Learning. 2016. pp. 612-621

[9] Dong C, Loy CC, He K, Tang X. Image super-resolution using deep convolutional networks. IEEE Transactions on Pattern Analysis and Machine Intelligence. 2015;**38**(2):295-307

[10] Cybenko G. Approximation by superpositions of a sigmoidal function. Mathematics of Control, Signals, and Systems. 1992;**5**(4):455

[11] He K, Zhang X, Ren S, Sun J. Deep residual learning for image recognition. In: Proceedings of the IEEE conference on computer vision and pattern recognition. 2016. pp. 770-778

[12] He K, Zhang X, Ren S, Sun J. Identity mappings in deep residual networks. In: European Conference on Computer Vision. Cham: Springer; 2016. pp. 630-645

[13] Szegedy C, Liu W, Jia Y, Sermanet P, Reed S, Anguelov D, et al. Going deeper with convolutions. In: Proceedings of the IEEE Conference on Computer Vision and Pattern Recognition. 2015. pp. 1-9

[14] Szegedy C, Vanhoucke V, Ioffe S, Shlens J, Wojna Z. Rethinking the inception architecture for computer vision. In: Proceedings of the IEEE Conference on Computer Vision and Pattern Recognition. 2016. pp. 2818-2826

[15] Sabour S, Frosst N, Hinton GE. Dynamic routing between capsules. In: Advances in Neural Information Processing Systems. 2017. pp. 3856-3866

[16] Hinton GE, Sabour S, Frosst N. Matrix capsules with EM routing. In: International Conference on Learning Representations. 2018

[17] Kosiorek A, Sabour S, Teh YW, Hinton GE. Stacked capsule autoencoders. In: Advances in Neural Information Processing Systems. 2019. pp. 15512-15522

[18] Russakovsky O, Deng J, Su H, Krause J, Satheesh S, Ma S, et al. Imagenet large scale visual recognition challenge. International Journal of Computer Vision. 2015;**115**(3):211-252

[19] Simonyan K, Zisserman A. Very Deep Convolutional Networks for Large-Scale Image Recognition. arXiv preprint arXiv:1409.1556. September 4, 2014

[20] Long J, Shelhamer E, Darrell T. Fully convolutional networks for semantic segmentation. In: Proceedings of the IEEE Conference on Computer Vision and Pattern Recognition. 2015. pp. 3431-3440

[21] Kingma DP, Welling M. Auto-encoding variational bayes. arXiv preprint arXiv:1312.6114. December 20, 2013

[22] Im DI, Ahn S, Memisevic R, Bengio Y. Denoising criterion for variational auto-encoding framework. In: Thirty-First AAAI Conference on Artificial Intelligence. 2017

[23] Kingma DP, Mohamed S, Rezende DJ, Welling M. Semi-supervised learning with deep generative models. In: Advances in Neural Information Processing Systems. 2014. pp. 3581-3589

[24] Sohn K, Lee H, Yan X. Learning structured output representation using deep conditional generative models. In: Advances in Neural Information Processing Systems. 2015. pp. 3483-3491

[25] Goodfellow I, Pouget-Abadie J, Mirza M, Xu B, Warde-Farley D, Ozair S, et al. Generative adversarial nets. In: Advances in neural information processing systems. 2014. pp. 2672-2680

[26] Mirza M, Osindero S. Conditional Generative Adversarial Nets. arXiv preprint arXiv:1411.1784. November 6, 2014

[27] Denton EL, Chintala S, Fergus R. Deep generative image models using a laplacian pyramid of adversarial networks. In: Advances in Neural Information Processing Systems. 2015. pp. 1486-1494

[28] Radford A, Metz L, Chintala S. Unsupervised Representation Learning with Deep Convolutional Generative Adversarial Networks. arXiv preprint arXiv:1511.06434. November 19, 2015

[29] Donahue J, Krähenbühl P, Darrell T. Adversarial Feature Learning. arXiv preprint arXiv:1605.09782. May 31, 2016

[30] Odena A. Semi-Supervised Learning with Generative Adversarial Networks. arXiv preprint arXiv:1606.01583. June 5, 2016

[31] Chen X, Duan Y, Houthooft R, Schulman J, Sutskever I, Abbeel P. Infogan: Interpretable representation learning by information maximizing generative adversarial nets. In: Advances in Neural Information Processing Systems. 2016. pp. 2172-2180

[32] Zhao J, Mathieu M, LeCun Y. Energy-Based Generative Adversarial Network. arXiv preprint arXiv: 1609.03126. September 11, 2016

[33] Odena A, Olah C, Shlens J. Conditional image synthesis with auxiliary classifier gans. In: International Conference on Machine Learning. 2017. pp. 2642-2651

[34] Karras T, Aila T, Laine S, Lehtinen J. Progressive Growing of Gans for Improved Quality, Stability, and Variation. arXiv preprint arXiv: 1710.10196. October 27, 2017

[35] Brock A, Donahue J, Simonyan K. Large Scale Gan Training for High Fidelity Natural Image Synthesis. arXiv preprint arXiv:1809.11096. September 28, 2018

[36] Zhang H, Goodfellow I, Metaxas D, Odena A. Self-attention generative adversarial networks. In: International Conference on Machine Learning. 2019. pp. 7354-7363

[37] Kaneko T, Ushiku Y, Harada T. Label-noise robust generative adversarial networks. In: Proceedings of the IEEE Conference on Computer Vision and Pattern Recognition. 2019. pp. 2467-2476

[38] Gong X, Chang S, Jiang Y, Wang Z. Autogan: Neural architecture search for generative adversarial networks. In: Proceedings of the IEEE International Conference on Computer Vision. 2019. pp. 3224-3234

[39] Daras G, Odena A, Zhang H, Dimakis AG. Your local GAN: Designing two dimensional local attention mechanisms for generative models. In: Proceedings of the IEEE/CVF Conference on Computer Vision and Pattern Recognition. 2020. pp. 14531-14539

[40] Karnewar A, Wang O. Msg-gan: Multi-scale gradients for generative adversarial networks. In: Proceedings of the IEEE/CVF Conference on Computer Vision and Pattern Recognition. 2020. pp. 7799-7808

[41] Kullback S, Leibler RA. On information and sufficiency. The annals of mathematical statistics. 1951;**22**(1): 79-86

[42] Deng J, Dong W, Socher R, Li LJ, Li K, Fei-Fei L. Imagenet: A large-scale hierarchical image database. In: 2009 IEEE Conference on Computer Vision and Pattern Recognition. IEEE; 2009. pp. 248-255

[43] Redmon J, Divvala S, Girshick R, Farhadi A. You only look once: Unified, real-time object detection. In: Proceedings of the IEEE Conference on Computer Vision and Pattern Recognition. 2016. pp. 779-788

[44] Liu W, Anguelov D, Erhan D, Szegedy C, Reed S, Fu CY, et al. Ssd: Single shot multibox detector. In: European Conference on Computer Vision. Cham: Springer; 2016. pp. 21-37

[45] Toshev A, Szegedy C. Deeppose: Human pose estimation via deep neural networks. In: Proceedings of the IEEE Conference on Computer Vision and Pattern Recognition. 2014. pp. 1653-1660

[46] Carreira J, Agrawal P, Fragkiadaki K, Malik J. Human pose estimation with iterative error feedback. In: Proceedings of the IEEE Conference on Computer Vision and Pattern Recognition. 2016. pp. 4733-4742

[47] Tompson JJ, Jain A, LeCun Y, Bregler C. Joint training of a convolutional network and a graphical model for human pose estimation. In: Advances in Neural Information Processing Systems. 2014. pp. 1799-1807

[48] Chu X, Yang W, Ouyang W, Ma C, Yuille AL, Wang X. Multi-context attention for human pose estimation. In: Proceedings of the IEEE Conference on Computer Vision and Pattern Recognition. 2017. pp. 1831-1840

[49] Mao X, Shen C, Yang YB. Image restoration using very deep convolutional encoder-decoder networks with symmetric skip connections. In: Advances in Neural Information Processing Systems. 2016. pp. 2802-2810

[50] Zhang Y, Tian Y, Kong Y, Zhong B, Fu Y. Residual dense network for image restoration. IEEE Transactions on Pattern Analysis and Machine Intelligence. 2020

[51] Johnson J, Karpathy A, Fei-Fei L. Densecap: Fully convolutional localization networks for dense captioning. In: Proceedings of the IEEE Conference on Computer Vision and

Pattern Recognition. 2016. pp. 4565-4574

[52] Huang L, Wang W, Chen J, Wei XY. Attention on attention for image captioning. In: Proceedings of the IEEE International Conference on Computer Vision. 2019. pp. 4634-4643

[53] Sainath TN, Mohamed AR, Kingsbury B, Ramabhadran B. Deep convolutional neural networks for LVCSR. In: 2013 IEEE international conference on acoustics, speech and signal processing. IEEE; 2013. pp. 8614-8618

[54] Abdel-Hamid O, Mohamed AR, Jiang H, Deng L, Penn G, Yu D. Convolutional neural networks for speech recognition. IEEE/ACM Transactions on audio, speech, and language processing. 2014;**22**(10): 1533-1545

[55] Amodei D, Ananthanarayanan S, Anubhai R, Bai J, Battenberg E, Case C, et al. Deep speech 2: End-to-end speech recognition in english and mandarin. In: International Conference on Machine Learning. 2016. pp. 173-182

[56] Zhang Y, Pezeshki M, Brakel P, Zhang S, Bengio CL, Courville A. Towards End-to-End Speech Recognition with Deep Convolutional Neural Networks. arXiv preprint arXiv: 1701.02720. January 10, 2017

[57] Souly N, Spampinato C, Shah M. Semi supervised semantic segmentation using generative adversarial network. In: Proceedings of the IEEE International Conference on Computer Vision. 2017. pp. 5688-5696

[58] Frid-Adar M, Diamant I, Klang E, Amitai M, Goldberger J, Greenspan H. GAN-based synthetic medical image augmentation for increased CNN performance in liver lesion classification. Neurocomputing. 2018; **321**:321-331

[59] Isola P, Zhu JY, Zhou T, Efros AA. Image-to-image translation with conditional adversarial networks. In: Proceedings of the IEEE Conference on Computer Vision and Pattern Recognition. 2017. pp. 1125-1134

[60] Zhu JY, Park T, Isola P, Efros AA. Unpaired image-to-image translation using cycle-consistent adversarial networks. In: Proceedings of the IEEE International Conference on Computer Vision. 2017. pp. 2223-2232

[61] Reed S, Akata Z, Yan X, Logeswaran L, Schiele B, Lee H. Generative Adversarial Text to Image Synthesis. arXiv preprint arXiv: 1605.05396. May 17, 2016

[62] Zhang H, Xu T, Li H, Zhang S, Wang X, Huang X, et al. Stackgan: Text to photo-realistic image synthesis with stacked generative adversarial networks. In: Proceedings of the IEEE International Conference on Computer Vision. 2017. pp. 5907-5915

[63] Ledig C, Theis L, Huszár F, Caballero J, Cunningham A, Acosta A, et al. Photo-realistic single image super-resolution using a generative adversarial network. In: Proceedings of the IEEE Conference on Computer Vision and Pattern Recognition. 2017. pp. 4681-4690

[64] Pathak D, Krahenbuhl P, Donahue J, Darrell T, Efros AA. Context encoders: Feature learning by inpainting. In: Proceedings of the IEEE Conference on Computer Vision and Pattern Recognition. 2016. pp. 2536-2544

[65] Yeh RA, Chen C, Yian Lim T, Schwing AG, Hasegawa-Johnson M, Do MN. Semantic image inpainting with deep generative models. In: Proceedings of the IEEE Conference on Computer Vision and Pattern Recognition. 2017. pp. 5485-5493

[66] Li Y, Liu S, Yang J, Yang MH. Generative face completion. In:

Proceedings of the IEEE Conference on Computer Vision and Pattern Recognition. 2017. pp. 3911-3919

[67] Xu N, Price B, Cohen S, Huang T. Deep image matting. In: Proceedings of the IEEE Conference on Computer Vision and Pattern Recognition. 2017. pp. 2970-2979

[68] Lutz S, Amplianitis K, Smolic A. Alphagan: Generative Adversarial Networks for Natural Image Matting. arXiv preprint arXiv:1807.10088. July 26, 2018

Chapter 3

Transfer Learning and Deep Domain Adaptation

Wen Xu, Jing He and Yanfeng Shu

Abstract

Transfer learning is an emerging technique in machine learning, by which we can solve a new task with the knowledge obtained from an old task in order to address the lack of labeled data. In particular deep domain adaptation (a branch of transfer learning) gets the most attention in recently published articles. The intuition behind this is that deep neural networks usually have a large capacity to learn representation from one dataset and part of the information can be further used for a new task. In this research, we firstly present the complete scenarios of transfer learning according to the domains and tasks. Secondly, we conduct a comprehensive survey related to deep domain adaptation and categorize the recent advances into three types based on implementing approaches: fine-tuning networks, adversarial domain adaptation, and sample-reconstruction approaches. Thirdly, we discuss the details of these methods and introduce some typical real-world applications. Finally, we conclude our work and explore some potential issues to be further addressed.

Keywords: transfer learning, deep domain adaptation, fine-tuning, adversarial domain adaptation, sample-reconstruction

1. Introduction

Inspired by the biological neurons, deep neural networks are well known for their ability to learn data representation from a huge amount of labeled data such as the famous convolutional neural networks (CNNs). Specifically, given a specific task such as image classification, we usually need to train a deep neural network from scratch with enough training data so that our model can achieve acceptable performance. However, sufficient training data for a new task is not always available as manually collecting and annotating data are labor-intensive and expensive. Especially in some specific domains such as healthcare, a privacy concern is also raised. Meanwhile, training a deep network with a large dataset is usually time-consuming and involves huge computational resources. Intuitively, it is not realistic and practical to learn from zero, because the real way we humans learn is that we usually try to solve a new task based on the knowledge obtained from past experiences. For example, once we have learned a programming language (e.g., Java), we can easily learn a new one (e.g., Python) as the basic programming fundamentals are the same.

Transfer Learning is an inspiring method that can help apply the knowledge gained from a source task to a new/target task. Specifically, the goal of transfer learning is to obtain some transferable representations between the source domain and target domain and utilize the stored knowledge to improve the performance on the target task. Note that transfer learning is an extensive research topic that involves many learning methods. In particular, deep domain adaptation gets the most attention in recent years among these methods. Therefore, after briefly introducing the transfer learning in this research, we pay our attention to analyzing and discussing the recent advances in deep domain adaptation.

The rest of this chapter is structured as follows. In Section 2, we give an overview and specific definitions of transfer learning. In Section 3, we summarize the main approaches for deep domain adaptation. In Section 4, 5 and 6, we discuss the details for conducting deep domain adaptation. The recent applications based on deep domain adaptation methods are also introduced in Section 7. Finally, we conclude this research and discuss future trends in Section 8.

2. Overview

We first give some notations and definitions which match those from the survey paper written by Pan et al. [1], and these notations are also widely adopted in many other survey papers such as [2, 3].

Definition 1 (**Domain** [1]) Given a specific dataset $X = \{X_1, \dots, X_n\} \in \mathcal{X}$, where $\mathcal{X}$ denotes the feature space, and a marginal probability distribution on the dataset $P(X)$. A domain can be defined as $\mathcal{D} = \{\mathcal{X}, P(X)\}$. Therefore, a domain consists of two components: the feature space and the marginal probability distribution on the dataset.

Definition 2 (**Task** [1]) Given a specific dataset $X = \{X_1, \dots, X_n\} \in \mathcal{X}$ and their labels $Y = \{Y_1, \dots, Y_n\} \in \mathcal{Y}$, where $\mathcal{Y}$ denotes the label space. A task can be defined as $\mathcal{T} = \{\mathcal{Y}, \mathcal{F}(X)\}$, where $\mathcal{F}$ is an objective predictive function to learn, which can be seen as a conditional distribution $P(Y|X)$.

Definition 3 (**Transfer Learning** [1]) Given a source domain $\mathcal{D}_s$ and its corresponding task $\mathcal{T}_s$, where the learned function $\mathcal{F}_s$ can be interpreted as some knowledge obtained in $\mathcal{D}_s$ and $\mathcal{T}_s$. Our goal is to get the target predictive function $\mathcal{F}_t$ for target task $\mathcal{T}_t$ with target domain $\mathcal{D}_t$. Transfer learning aims to help improve the performance of $\mathcal{F}_t$ by utilizing the knowledge $\mathcal{F}_s$, where $\mathcal{D}_s \neq \mathcal{D}_t$ or $\mathcal{T}_s \neq \mathcal{T}_t$.

In short, transfer learning can be simply denoted as

$$\mathcal{D}_s, \mathcal{T}_s \rightarrow \mathcal{D}_t, \mathcal{T}_t \tag{1}$$

Transfer learning is a very broad research subject in machine learning. In this research, we mainly focus on transfer learning based on deep neural networks (i.e., deep learning). Therefore, as shown in **Figure 1**, based on $\mathcal{D}_s \neq \mathcal{D}_t$ or $\mathcal{T}_s \neq \mathcal{T}_t$, we can have three scenarios when applying transfer learning. Note that when $\mathcal{D}_s = \mathcal{D}_t$ and $\mathcal{T}_s = \mathcal{T}_t$, the problem becomes a traditional deep learning task. In such case, a dataset is usually divided into a training dataset $\mathcal{D}_s$ and a test training dataset $\mathcal{D}_t$, then we can train a neural network $\mathcal{F}$ on $\mathcal{D}_s$ and apply the pre-trained model $\mathcal{F}$ to $\mathcal{D}_t$.

When $\mathcal{D}_s = \mathcal{D}_t$ and $\mathcal{T}_s \neq \mathcal{T}_t$, transfer learning is usually transformed into a multi-task learning problem. Since the source domain and the target domain share the same feature space, we can utilize one giant neural network to solve different types of tasks at the same time. For example, multi-task learning is widely used in the autopilot system. Given an input image, we can utilize a deep neural network that has enough capacity to recognize the cars, the pedestrians, traffic signs, and the locations of these objectives in the image.

When $\mathcal{D}_s \neq \mathcal{D}_t$ and $\mathcal{T}_s = \mathcal{T}_t$, deep domain adaptation technique is usually used to transfer the knowledge from the source to the target. In general, the goal of domain adaptation is to learn a mapping function $\mathcal{F}$ to reduce the domain

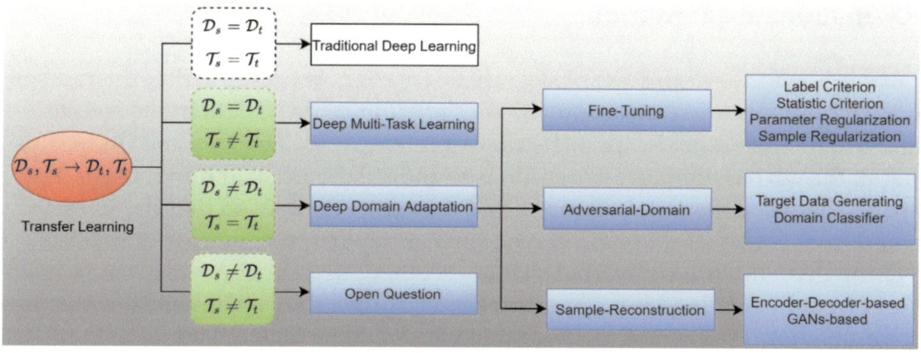

Figure 1.
Hierarchically-structured taxonomy of transfer learning in this survey.

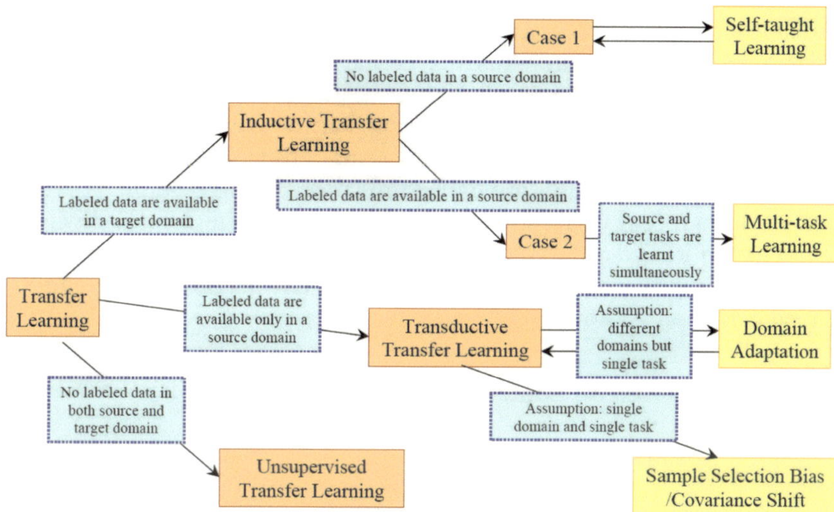

Figure 2.
Categorization of transfer learning based on labels. (The image is from Pan [1]).

divergence between $\mathcal{D}_s$ and $\mathcal{D}_t$ including distribution shift and different feature spaces. Formally, the definition of domain adaptation can be defined as.

Definition 4 (**Domain Adaptation**) Given a source domain $\mathcal{D}_s$ for task $\mathcal{T}_s$ and a target domain $\mathcal{D}_t$ for task $\mathcal{T}_t$, where $\mathcal{D}_s \neq \mathcal{D}_t$. Domain adaptation aims to learn a predictive function $\mathcal{F}_t$ so that the knowledge obtained from $\mathcal{D}_s$ and $\mathcal{T}_s$ can be used for enhancing $\mathcal{F}_t$. In other words, the domain divergence is adapted in $\mathcal{F}_t$.

When $\mathcal{D}_s \neq \mathcal{D}_t$ and $\mathcal{T}_s \neq \mathcal{T}_t$, transfer learning should be conducted carefully. If the data in source domain $\mathcal{D}_s$ is very different from that in target domain $\mathcal{D}_t$, brute-force transfer may hurt the performance of predictive function $\mathcal{F}_t$, not to mention the scenario when source task $\mathcal{T}_s$ and target task $\mathcal{T}_t$ are also different. From a literature review of deep learning, we notice that there is little research in this scenario and it is still an open question.

In summary, the above definitions give us the answer to what to transfer, and the four scenarios demonstrate the research issue of when to transfer. As shown in **Figure 2**, in contrast to the categorization of transfer learning that is introduced in the survey paper [1], our discussions mainly focus on transfer learning in deep neural networks. In the following sections, we pay our attention to how to transfer. Specifically, we will introduce and summarize three main methods for deep domain adaptation.

3. Deep domain adaptation

According to the definition of domain adaptation, we assume that the tasks of the source domain and target domain are the same, and the data in the source domain and target domain are different but related (i.e., $\mathcal{D}_s \neq \mathcal{D}_t$ and $\mathcal{T}_s = \mathcal{T}_t$). In general, the goal of domain adaptation is to reduce the domain distribution discrepancy between the source domain and the target domain so that the knowledge learned from the source domain can be further applied to the target domain.

Compared with the traditional shallow method, deep domain adaptation mainly focuses on utilizing deep neural networks to improve the performance of the predictive function $\mathcal{F}_t$. Formally, a neural network can be denoted as

$$\hat{Y} = \mathcal{F}(X; \Theta) \tag{2}$$

where $\mathcal{F}$ denotes a neural network and Θ is a set of parameters, $\hat{Y}$ represents the predicted label of input X. The deep neural architecture is usually specifically designed to learn representation with back-propagation from the source and target data for domain adaptation. The intuition behind domain adaptation is that we can find some domain-invariant schemes or sharing features from related datasets. In other words, we ensure that the internal representations learned from related domains in deep neural networks are indiscriminating. In this section, based on the published works in recent years, we discuss how to reduce the domain divergence in deep neural networks and categorize deep domain adaptation approaches into three main ways, including fine-tuning networks, domain-adversarial learning, and sample-reconstruction approach.

3.1 Categorization based on implementing approaches

3.1.1 Fine-tuning networks

A natural way to reduce the domain shift is to fine-tune the pre-trained networks with the data in the target domain, as the past researches show that the internal representations of deep convolutional neural networks learned from large datasets, such as ImageNet, can be effectively used for solving a variety of tasks in computer vision. Specifically, for a pre-trained model such as VGG [4] or ResNet [5], we can keep its earlier layers fixed/frozen and only fine-tune the weights in the high-level portion of the network by continuing back-propagation. Or we can fine-tune all the layers if needed. The main idea behind this is that the learned low-level representations in the earlier layers mainly consist of generic features such as the edge detector. During fine-tuning the networks, the discrepancy between the source domain and target domain is usually measured by a criterion such as class labels based criterion, and statistic criterion. Instead of directly using the measurement as a criterion to adjust networks, regularization techniques can also be used for fine-tuning, which mainly includes parameter regularization and sample regularization.

3.1.2 Adversarial domain adaptation

Generative Adversarial Networks (GANs) are a promising method and get the most attention due to its unsupervised learning approach and the flexibility of generator design. Since the first version of GANs is proposed by Goodfellow et al. [6], many variants based on it have been proposed for solving different types of tasks. Specifically, there are normally two networks in GANs, namely a generator and a discriminator. The generator can synthesize fake examples from an input space called latent space and the discriminator can distinguish real samples from fake. By alternately training these two players, both of them can enhance their abilities. The fundamental idea behind GANs is that we want the data distribution learned by the generator is close to the true data distribution. And this is very similar to the principle of domain adaptation, which is that the learned data distribution between the source domain and the target domain is close to each other (i.e., domain confusion). For example, a representative work related to adversarial domain adaptation is [7], in which a generalized framework based on GANs is introduced. Instead of using GANs for domain-adversarial learning, a more simple but powerful method is to add a domain classifier into a general deep network for encouraging domain confusion [8].

3.1.3 Data-reconstruction approaches

Data-reconstruction approaches are a type of deep domain adaptation method that utilizes the deep encoder-decoder architectures, where the encoder networks are used for the tasks and the decoder network can be treated as an auxiliary task to ensure that the learned features between the source domain and target domain are invariant or sharing. There are mainly two types of methods to conduct data reconstruction: (1) A typical way is by utilizing an encoder-decoder deep network for domain adaptation such as [9]; (2) Another way is to conduct sample reconstruction based on GANs such as cycle GANs [10].

3.1.4 Hybrid approaches

In general, the core idea of deep domain adaptation is to learn indiscriminating internal representations from the source domain and target domain with deep neural networks. Therefore, we can combine different kinds of approaches discussed above to enhance the overall performance. For example, in [11], they adopt both the encoder-decoder reconstruction method and the statistic criterion method.

3.2 Categorization based on learning methods

Based on whether there are labels in the target domain datasets, we can further divide the above approaches into supervised learning and unsupervised learning. Note that the unsupervised learning methods can be generalized and applied to semi-supervised cases, therefore, we mainly discuss these two methods in this research. **Table 1** shows the categorization of deep domain adaptation based on whether the labels are needed in the target domain. A similar categorization is also introduced in [12].

3.3 Categorization based on data space

In some survey papers, the domain adaptation methods can also be categorized into two main methods based on the similarity of data space. (1) Homogeneous domain adaptation represents that the source data space and the target data space is the same (i.e., $\mathcal{X}_s = \mathcal{X}_t$). E.g., the source dataset consists of some images of cars from open public datasets, and the images of cars in the target dataset are manually collected from the real world. (2) Heterogeneous domain adaptation represents that the datasets are from different data space (i.e., $\mathcal{X}_s \neq \mathcal{X}_t$). E.g., text vs. images. **Figure 3** presents the topology that is introduced in [12].

		Supervised	Unsupervised
Fine-tuning	Label criterion	✓	
	Statistic criterion		✓
	Parameter regularization	✓	✓
	Sample regularization	✓	✓
Adversarial-domain	Domain classifier		✓
	Target data generating		✓
Sample-reconstruction	Encoder-decoder-based		✓
	GAN-based		✓

Table 1.
Categorization of deep domain adaptation based on whether the labels in the target domain are available.

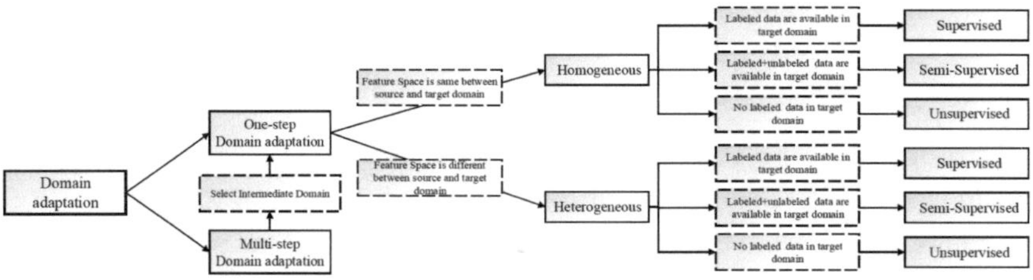

Figure 3.
Categorization of domain adaptation based on feature space. (The image is from Wang [12]).

4. Fine-tuning networks

In the last section, we categorize the main methods to conduct domain adaptation with deep neural networks and give some high-level information. In this section, we firstly discuss the details of four approaches for fine-tuning networks in **Table 1**.

4.1 Label criterion

The most basic approach to conduct domain adaptation is to fine-tune a pre-trained network with labeled data from the target domain. Hence, we assume that the labels in the target dataset are available and we can utilize a supervised learning approach to adjust the weights/parameters in the network. Based on the definition of the task, our target task $\mathcal{T}_t$ based on label criterion approach is

$$\mathcal{T}_t = \mathcal{L}(Y_t, \hat{Y}_t) = \mathcal{L}(Y_t, \mathcal{F}_t(X_t; \Theta)) \tag{3}$$

where $\mathcal{L}$ denotes a loss function, such as the cross-entropy loss $\mathcal{L}(Y, \hat{Y}) = -Ylog(\hat{Y}) - (1 - Y)\,log\,(1 - \hat{Y})$, which is commonly used in many works. Note that Θ is a set of parameters which is normally initialized with weights from the pre-trained model.

As discussed in Section 3.1, a question is that how many layers in the neural network we should freeze. In general, there are two main factors that can influence the fine-tuning procedure: the size of the target dataset and its similarity to the source domain. Based on the two factors, some common rules of thumb are introduced in [13]. One typical work is [14], in which a unified supervised method for deep domain adaptation is proposed. Another problem is that what if there are no labels in the target dataset. Therefore, an unsupervised learning method must be applied to the target dataset for domain confusion.

4.2 Statistic criterion

From the definition of domain adaptation, we see that the fundamental goal is to reduce the domain divergence between the source domain and target domain so that the function $\mathcal{F}_t$ can achieve good performance on the target domain. Therefore, it's important and valuable to use a criterion to measure the divergence between different domains. In other words, we need to have a measurement of the difference of probability distributions from different datasets.

Maximum Mean Discrepancy (MMD) [15] is a well-known criterion that is widely adopted in deep domain adaptation such as [16, 17]. Specifically, MMD computes the mean squared difference between the two datasets, which can be defined as

$$\begin{aligned}\mathcal{D}_{MMD}(X^s, X^t) &= \left\| \frac{1}{n}\sum_{i=1}^{n}\phi(x_i^s) - \frac{1}{m}\sum_{j=1}^{m}\phi(x_i^t)\right\|^2 \\ &= \frac{1}{n^2}\sum_{i=1}^{n}\sum_{j=1}^{n}\phi(x_i^s)^{\mathrm{T}}\phi\left(x_j^s\right) - \frac{2}{nm}\sum_{i=1}^{n}\sum_{j=1}^{m}\phi(x_i^s)^{\mathrm{T}}\phi(x_i^t) + \frac{1}{m^2}\sum_{i=1}^{m}\sum_{j=1}^{m}\phi(x_i^t)^{\mathrm{T}}\phi\left(x_j^t\right) \\ &= \frac{1}{n^2}\sum_{i=1}^{n}\sum_{j=1}^{n}k\left(x_i^s, x_j^s\right) - \frac{2}{nm}\sum_{i=1}^{n}\sum_{j=1}^{m}k\left(x_i^s, x_j^t\right) + \frac{1}{m^2}\sum_{i=1}^{m}\sum_{j=1}^{m}k\left(x_i^t, x_j^t\right)\end{aligned} \tag{4}$$

where $\phi()$ denotes the feature space map. In practice, we can use the kernel method $k()$ to make MMD be computed easily (i.e., Gaussian kernel).

$\mathcal{H}$-divergence [18] is a more general theory to measure the domain divergence, which is defined as

$$d_{\mathcal{H}}(\mathcal{D}_s, \mathcal{D}_t) = 2\sup_{h\in\mathcal{H}}\left|\Pr_{x_s\sim\mathcal{D}_s}[h(x_s) = 1] - \Pr_{x_t\sim\mathcal{D}_t}[h(x_t) = 1]\right| \tag{5}$$

where $h \in \mathcal{H}$ is a binary classifier (i.e., hypothesis). For example, in [19], domain-adversarial networks are proposed based on this statistic criterion (note that this method can belong to the approach of domain-adversarial learning).

4.3 Parameter regularization

Note that for fine-tuning networks with the label criterion or the statistic criterion, the weights in the networks are usually shared between the source domain and target domain. In contrast to these methods, some researchers argue that the weights for each domain should be related but not shared. Based on this idea, the authors in [20] propose a two-stream architecture with a weight regularization method. Two types of regularizers are introduced: L_2 norm or in an exponential form.

$$\begin{aligned} r_w\left(\theta_j^s, \theta_j^t\right) &= \left\|a_j\theta_j^s + b_j - \theta_j^t\right\| \\ or &= exp\left(\left\|a_j\theta_j^s + b_j - \theta_j^t\right\|\right) - 1\end{aligned} \tag{6}$$

where a_j and b_j are different parameters in each layer. Rather than using two networks for domain adaptation, in [21], they introduce a domain guided method to drop some weights in the networks directly.

4.4 Sample regularization

Alternatively, instead of adapting the parameters in the networks, we can re-weight the data in each layer of feed-forward neural networks. The typical method to reduce internal covariate shit in deep neural networks is to conduct batch normalization during training [22].

$$\hat{x}_i = \gamma \frac{x_i - \mu}{\sqrt{\sigma^2 + \varepsilon}} + \beta \tag{7}$$

Note that x_i usually denotes the hidden activation of input sample x_i in each layer of a neural network (e.g., the output feature map of each convolutional layer). $\mu = \frac{1}{B}\sum_{i=1}^{B} x_i$ and $\sigma = \frac{1}{B}\sum_{i=1}^{B}(x_i - \mu)^2$. B is the batch size, γ and β are two hyper-parameters to learn. Based on this method, [23] propose a revised method for practical domain adaptation. And in [24], researchers adopt instance normalization for stylization.

5. Adversarial domain adaptation

Instead of directly fine-tuning networks, adversarial domain adaptation is an appealing alternative to unsupervised learning. It mainly addresses the problem that there are abundant labeled data in the source domain but sparse/limited unlabeled samples in the target domain. The core idea of the adversarial domain adaptation is based on GANs. Specifically, a generalized architecture to implement this idea is proposed in [7]. In this section, we detail two main ideas: target data generating and domain classifier.

5.1 Target data generating

To overcome the limitation of sparse unlabeled data, target data generating is an approach to directly generate samples with labels for the target domain so that we can utilize them to train a classifier for the new task. One representative work is the CoGANs [25], in which there are two GANs involved: one for processing the labeled data in the source domain and another for processing the unlabeled data in the target domain. Part of the weights in the two generators is shared/tied in order to reduce the domain divergence. In addition to two discriminators for classifying the fake and real samples, there is also an extra classifier to classify the samples based on the information of labels in the source domain. By jointly training these two GANs, we can generate unlimited pairs of data, in which each pair consists of a synthetic source sample and a synthetic target sample and each pair shares the same label. Therefore, after finishing jointly training the two GANs, the pre-trained extra classifier is the function $\mathcal{F}_t$ that we need for solving the new task. Similar work can also be found in [26], in which a transformation in the pixel space is introduced.

In summary, target data generating is a domain adaptation approach that focuses on generating target data, which can also be treated as an auxiliary task to reduce domain shift by a weight sharing mechanism between two GANs. The main disadvantage is that the training cost for generating synthesized samples with two GANs is expensive especially when the target datasets consist of large-size samples such as high-resolution images.

5.2 Domain classifier

Instead of directly synthesizing labeled data for domain adaptation, an alternative way is to add an extra domain classifier to enough domain confusion. The role of domain classifier is similar to that of the discriminator in GANs, it can distinguish the data between the source domain and target domain (the discriminator in GANs is responsible for recognizing the fake from the real data). With the help of an adversarial learning approach, the domain classifier can help the network learn domain-invariant representation from the source domain and the target domain. In other words, the trained model can be directly used for the target/new task.

Therefore, the key is how to conduct adversarial learning with the domain classifier. In [8], a gradient reversal layer (GRL) before domain classifier is introduced to maximize the gradients for encouraging domain confusion (we normally minimize the gradients for reducing the scalar value of a loss function). In [27], a domain confusion loss is proposed beside the domain classifier loss.

6. Sample-reconstruction approaches

The core idea of the data-reconstruction approach is to utilize the reconstruction as an auxiliary task for encouraging domain confusion in an unsupervised manner. In this section, we discuss two types of approaches that are mainly addressed in recent years, including the encoder-decoder-based method and the GANs-based method.

6.1 Encoder-decoder-based approaches

To reconstruct the samples, the basic method is that we can adopt an auto-encoder framework, in which there is an encoder network and decoder network. The encoder can map an input sample into a hidden representation and the decoder can reconstruct the input sample based on the hidden representation. In particular, the encoder-decoder networks for domain adaptation typically involve a shared encoder between the source domain and target domain so that the encoder can learn some domain-invariant representation. An earlier work can be found in [9], in which the stacked denoising auto-encoder is adopted for sentiment classification.

Recently, a typical work called deep reconstruction-classification networks is introduced in [11], in which the encoder and decoder are both implemented with convolutional networks. Specifically, the convolutional encoder is used for supervised classification of the labeled data from the source domain. Meanwhile, it also maps the unlabeled data from the target domain into hidden representation, which is further decoded by the convolutional encoder for reconstructing the input. By jointly training these networks with the data from the source and target domains, the shared encoder can learn some common representations from both datasets, which results in domain adaptation. Other similar work based on auto-encoder can also be found in [11, 28].

6.2 GAN-based approaches

Traditionally, the GANs [6] consists of a generator and discriminator, where the generator can be seen as a decoder network which can decode some random noise into a fake sample and the discriminator can be treated as an encoder network which is used to encode the sample into some high-level features for classification (i.e., fake or real). Instead of just using a decoder network as the generator, a typical work known as Cycle GANs is proposed in [10], in which the generator is implemented with an encoder-decoder network. Specifically, this encoder-decoder generator is used for dual learning: $G(x_s) \rightarrow x_t$ and $F(x_t) \rightarrow x_s$. And the discriminator also has two roles: to distinguish between the fake x_t and real x_t, and to distinguish between the fake x_s and real x_s. By alternatively training these two players in GANs, the encoder-decoder generator can lean a reversible mapping function. In other words, the domain-invariant features are obtained from two different datasets. However, one remaining problem is that the encoder-decoder network usually consists of millions of parameters, with enough capacity, it can map an input image from the source domain to any random image which is close to the target domain. Therefore, in addition to using the standard adversarial loss for training the GANs, the consistency loss (i.e., L1 norm) is also proposed to make sure that $F(G(x)) \approx x$.

$$\mathcal{L}_{cyc}(G,F) = \mathbb{E}_{x_s \sim data(x_s)} \|F(G(x_s)) - x_s\|_1 + \mathbb{E}_{x_t \sim data(x_t)} \|F(G(x_t)) - x_t\|_1 \tag{8}$$

where $G(x_s)$ denotes fake x_t and $F(G(x_s))$ is reconstructed x_s (i.e., $F(x_t) \rightarrow x_s$). Inspired by the Cycle GANs, many variants based on encoder-decoder generator are proposed for domain adaptation, such as the Disco GANs [29] and the Dual GANs [30].

7. Applications

As shown in **Figure 1**, the scope of transfer learning is far beyond traditional machine learning. Theoretically, the problems addressed by deep learning can also be solved by transfer learning. In this section, we narrow the discussion to the typical real-world applications based on deep domain adaptation. In Section 7.1, we summarize the most methods discussed above for computer vision. In Section 7.2, we discuss the applications beyond the context of image processing, including natural language processing, speech recognition and other real-world applications based on processing time-serial data.

7.1 Applications in computer vision

7.1.1 Image classification and recognition

Classification is a fundamental and most basic problem in machine learning, most of the above methods are introduced to address this problem. Therefore, we pay our attention to the advances that deep domain adaptation can bring for image classification, rather than repeatedly introducing them. Probably the most well-known example is fine-tuning a giant network that is pre-trained with the ImageNet dataset for real-world applications such as pet recognition. Despite the fact that manually collecting data is time-consuming and expensive, the data collected from the real-world is usually imbalanced (e.g., there are only 100 images of class A but 10,000 images of class B). If we train a classifier from scratch, the performance can be poor because it cannot learn enough knowledge from the limited samples (e.g., class A). However, if we utilize a pre-trained model based on the well-collected ImageNet and fine-tune it, the problem caused by an imbalance dataset will be reduced because the model has already obtained rich knowledge from the source domain.

Another typical real-world application that we can gain benefits from domain adaptation is face recognition. A general approach to solve this problem is to train a model based on a dataset of labeled face images. In contrast, the large-scale unlabeled video datasets are always available. However, the divergence of data in the video is usually limited and there remains a clear gap between these two different domains. In order to utilize the rich information from video and overcome these challenges, the authors in [31] propose a framework for face recognition in unlabeled video based on the adversarial domain adaptation approach.

7.1.2 Object detection

The recent object detection methods are mainly driven by two approaches: Faster R-CNN [32] and YOLO [33]. Specifically, two tasks are mainly involved in object detection: The first one is to detect whether there are objects in an input image (i.e., to output the bounding box of each object in the image); Meanwhile, the object in each bounding box is also classified. Object detection is a very common learning task in many real-world applications such as intelligent surveillance systems [34]. By utilizing domain adaptation approaches for the new task of object detection in the wild, the Domain Adaptive Faster R-CNN is introduced in [35]. And the core idea is also to utilize domain classifier with GRL to encourage domain confusion (i.e., in Section 5.2). Another recent similar work is also discussed in [36], in which the GRL is also adopted and the process of conducting domain adaptation is divided into two stages called progress domain adaptation.

7.1.3 Image segmentation

The convolutional encoder-decoder architecture has achieved great success for image segmentation in recent years. Specifically, given an input image, the convolutional encoder-decoder network can map this image into a pixel-level classification image (i.e., each pixel is classified with a label). The problem of domain shifts can also appear in this task, which results in poor performance on a new domain. In [37], the researchers introduce a domain adversarial learning method which includes both global and category-specific techniques. They argue that two factors can cause domain shift: the global changes between the two distinct domains and the category-specific changes. (i.e., the distribution of cars from two different cities may be different.) Based on this assumption, two new loss functions are introduced, one is used for reducing the global distribution shift between the source images and target images and the other is used for adapting the category-specific divergence between the target images and the transferring label statistics. Instead of just using a simple adversarial objective, the authors in [38] propose an iterative optimization procedure based on GANs for addressing domain shift.

7.1.4 Image-to-image translation

As mentioned in Section 6.2, Cycle GANs [10] is a typical method for image-to-image translation based on deep domain adaptation. In general, image-to-image translation denotes that we can map an image from the source domain to the target domain and vice versa. One real task that is also addressed in Cycle GANs is the style transfer application. To our best knowledge, the algorithm of neural style transfer is firstly proposed in [39], the core idea in this paper is how to define the content loss and style loss between the source data and the target data. Actually, it can be treated as a statistic criterion approach which is discussed in Section 4.2. In the paper of demystifying neural style transfer [40], the authors show that matching Gram matrices (i.e., style loss) is equivalent to minimize the MMD (i.e., Eq. 4). Based on this argument, they introduce several style transfer methods by utilizing different types of kernel functions in the MMD and achieve impressive results.

7.1.5 Image caption

An interesting but challenging task is to utilize deep neural networks to describe an input image with natural language, which is well known as the image caption. Specifically, the goal of image caption is to learn a mapping function $\mathcal{F}_t$, so that we can get $\mathcal{F}_t(Image) \rightarrow Text$ and vice versa. Note that there are two different data space involved in this task: a dataset with images vs. a dataset with text. Therefore, based on the categorization methods which are discussed in Section 3.3, image caption belongs to heterogeneous domain adaptation. A general method to implement this idea is to utilize a CNN-RNN architecture (i.e., recurrent neural network), where the CNN is used for encoding an input image to some hidden representation and the RNN can decode the representation to some sentences which can describe the content of this image. In particular, the CNN is usually pre-trained based on the ImageNet and then we can re-train it in the CNN-RNN [41].

When we apply an image-caption model which is trained from image dataset A on image dataset B, the performance will degrade due to the distribution change or domain shift of two datasets. To address this problem, the work in [42] introduces an adversarial learning method to address unpaired data in the target domain for image caption (i.e., adversarial domain adaptation approach in Section 5). In [43], the authors propose a dual learning method for addressing this problem, which involves two steps: (1) A CNN-RNN model is trained with sufficient labeled data in the source domain. (2) The model is then fine-tuned with limited target data. The core idea of dual learning mechanism involved a reverse mapping process: the model firstly maps an input target image to text (i.e., $CNN - RNN(Image) \rightarrow Text$) and the text is then mapped back to an image by a generator network, which is further distinguished by a discriminator network. Therefore, the work in [43] belongs to sample-reconstruction approach (i.e., in Section 6).

7.2 Applications beyond computer vision

7.2.1 Natural language processing

Deep domain adaptation technique is also used for solving a variety of tasks in processing natural language. In [44], an effective domain mixing method for machine translation is introduced. The core idea is to jointly train domain discrimination and translation networks. The authors in [45] propose aspect-augmented adversarial networks for text classification. The main idea is to adopt a domain classifier, which has been discussed in Section 5.2. Recently, an interesting research area is to utilize neural models to automatically generate answers based on the input questions, which is also known as questions answering. However, the main challenge to train models is that it is usually difficult to collect a large dataset of labeled question-answer pairs. Therefore, domain adaptation is a natural choice to address this problem. E.g., in [46], a framework called generative domain-adaptive nets is introduced. Specifically, a generative model is used to generate questions from the unlabeled text for enhancing the model performance. Other applications of domain adaptation can also be found in sentence specificity prediction [47], where the specificity denotes the quality of a sentence that belongs to a specific subject.

7.2.2 Speech recognition

A typical real-world application is to transcribe speech into text, which is also known as automatic speech recognition. Domain adaptation is also suitable for addressing the training-testing mismatch of speech recognition that is caused by the shift of data distribution between different datasets. For example, a neural model trained on a manually collected dataset may generalize poorly in the real-world application of speech recognition due to the environmental noises. In [48], an adaptive teacher-student learning method is proposed for domain adaptation in speech recognition systems. In [49], the domain classifier that is discussed above is also adopted for robust speech recognition. Similar work can also be found in [50], in which the adversarial learning method for domain adaptation is also used for addressing the unseen recoding conditions.

7.2.3 Time-series data processing

Domain adaptation can also enhance the performance of processing many other time-series datasets such as healthcare time-series datasets [51], in which the authors present a variational recurrent adversarial method for domain adaptation. The main idea is to learn domain-invariant temporal latent representations of multivariate time-series data. Another real-world task that involves time-series data is to build diver assistant systems. In [52], an auxiliary domain classifier is also adopted to enhance the performance of recurrent neural networks for driving maneuvers anticipation. And the core idea in this paper is also to learn sharing features from different datasets by the domain classifier. An interesting work related to inertial information processing is introduced in [53], in which a novel framework called MotionTransformer is proposed for extracting domain-invariant features of raw sequences.

8. Conclusion

In this chapter, we firstly introduce the background and explain why transfer learning is important for helping learn real-world tasks. Then we give a strict definition of transfer learning and its scope. In particular, we pay our attention to deep domain adaptation, which is a subset of transfer learning and it mainly addresses the situation where we have different but related datasets for a common learning task. Next, we categorize the deep domain adaptation based on three aspects: the specific implementing approaches, the learning methods, and the data space. In general, deep domain adaptation is one type of method that mainly utilizes deep neural networks to reduce the domain shift or data distribution so that we can enhance the performance of the target task with the help of the knowledge obtained from the source domain. Specifically, we mainly discuss the recent advanced methods for domain adaptation from the deep learning community, including fine-tuning networks, adversarial domain adaptation, and data-reconstruction approaches. Finally, we introduce and summarize the typical real-world applications in computer vision from recently published articles, from which we can see that the unsupervised learning approach based on GANs gets the most attention. In addition, we discuss many other applications beyond the context of image processing. And we notice that many deep domain adaptation methods that are initially proposed for processing images are also suitable for addressing a variety of tasks in natural language processing, speech recognition, and time-series data processing.

Although deep domain adaptation has been successfully used for solving various types of tasks, we should be careful to conduct transfer learning, as brute-force transfer may hurt the performance of our model. The above applications mainly focus on homogeneous domain adaptation, which means that the data between the source domain and the target domain is related and we assume that deep neural networks can find some shared representation from these two domains. However, the data collected from real-world may not always meet this requirement. Therefore, the future challenge is how to apply a heterogeneous domain adaptation method effectively. From the above analyses, we notice that transfer learning has been mainly applied to a limited scale of applications. Therefore, more challenges are also needed to address in the future such as logical inference and graph neural networks based tasks.

Acknowledgements

This work is supported by China Scholarship Council and Data61 from CSIRO, Australia.

Conflict of interest

The authors declare no conflict of interest.

Author details

Wen Xu[1,2], Jing He[1*] and Yanfeng Shu[2]

1 Swinburne University of Technology, Australia

2 Data61, CSIRO, Australia

*Address all correspondence to: jinghe@swin.edu.au

References

[1] Pan SJ, Yang Q. A survey on transfer learning. IEEE Transactions on knowledge and data engineering. 2009 Oct 16;22(10):1345–59.

[2] Weiss K, Khoshgoftaar TM, Wang D. A survey of transfer learning. Journal of Big data. 2016 Dec 1;3(1):9.

[3] Zhang J, Li W, Ogunbona P. Transfer learning for cross-dataset recognition: a survey. arXiv preprint arXiv: 1705.04396. 2017 May.

[4] Simonyan K, Zisserman A. Very deep convolutional networks for large-scale image recognition. arXiv preprint arXiv: 1409.1556. 2014 Sep 4.

[5] He K, Zhang X, Ren S, Sun J. Deep residual learning for image recognition. InProceedings of the IEEE conference on computer vision and pattern recognition 2016 (pp. 770–778).

[6] Goodfellow I, Pouget-Abadie J, Mirza M, Xu B, Warde-Farley D, Ozair S, Courville A, Bengio Y. Generative adversarial nets. InAdvances in neural information processing systems 2014 (pp. 2672–2680).

[7] Tzeng E, Hoffman J, Saenko K, Darrell T. Adversarial discriminative domain adaptation. InProceedings of the IEEE conference on computer vision and pattern recognition 2017 (pp. 7167–7176).

[8] Ganin Y, Lempitsky V. Unsupervised domain adaptation by backpropagation. InInternational conference on machine learning 2015 Jun 1 (pp. 1180–1189).

[9] Ghifary M, Kleijn WB, Zhang M, Balduzzi D, Li W. Deep reconstruction-classification networks for unsupervised domain adaptation. InEuropean Conference on Computer Vision 2016 Oct 8 (pp. 597–613). Springer, Cham.

[10] Zhu JY, Park T, Isola P, Efros AA. Unpaired image-to-image translation using cycle-consistent adversarial networks. InProceedings of the IEEE international conference on computer vision 2017 (pp. 2223–2232).

[11] Bousmalis K, Trigeorgis G, Silberman N, Krishnan D, Erhan D. Domain separation networks. InAdvances in neural information processing systems 2016 (pp. 343–351).

[12] Wang M, Deng W. Deep visual domain adaptation: A survey. Neurocomputing. 2018 Oct 27;312: 135–53.

[13] Chu B, Madhavan V, Beijbom O, Hoffman J, Darrell T. Best practices for fine-tuning visual classifiers to new domains. InEuropean conference on computer vision 2016 Oct 8 (pp. 435–442). Springer, Cham.

[14] Motiian S, Piccirilli M, Adjeroh DA, Doretto G. Unified deep supervised domain adaptation and generalization. InProceedings of the IEEE International Conference on Computer Vision 2017 (pp. 5715–5725).

[15] Borgwardt KM, Gretton A, Rasch MJ, Kriegel HP, Schölkopf B, Smola AJ. Integrating structured biological data by kernel maximum mean discrepancy. Bioinformatics. 2006 Jul 15;22(14):e49–57.

[16] Long M, Zhu H, Wang J, Jordan MI. Unsupervised domain adaptation with residual transfer networks. InAdvances in neural information processing systems 2016 (pp. 136–144).

[17] Long M, Zhu H, Wang J, Jordan MI. Deep transfer learning with joint adaptation networks. InInternational conference on machine learning 2017 Jul 17 (pp. 2208–2217).

[18] Ben-David S, Blitzer J, Crammer K, Kulesza A, Pereira F, Vaughan JW. A theory of learning from different domains. Machine learning. 2010 May 1; 79(1–2):151–75.

[19] Ganin Y, Ustinova E, Ajakan H, Germain P, Larochelle H, Laviolette F, Marchand M, Lempitsky V. Domain-adversarial training of neural networks. The Journal of Machine Learning Research. 2016 Jan 1;17(1):2096–30.

[20] Rozantsev A, Salzmann M, Fua P. Beyond sharing weights for deep domain adaptation. IEEE transactions on pattern analysis and machine intelligence. 2018 Mar 8;41(4):801–14.

[21] Xiao T, Li H, Ouyang W, Wang X. Learning deep feature representations with domain guided dropout for person re-identification. InProceedings of the IEEE conference on computer vision and pattern recognition 2016 (pp. 1249–1258).

[22] Ioffe S, Szegedy C. Batch normalization: Accelerating deep network training by reducing internal covariate shift. arXiv preprint arXiv: 1502.03167. 2015 Feb 11.

[23] Li Y, Wang N, Shi J, Liu J, Hou X. Revisiting batch normalization for practical domain adaptation. arXiv preprint arXiv:1603.04779. 2016 Mar 15.

[24] Ulyanov D, Vedaldi A, Lempitsky V. Improved texture networks: Maximizing quality and diversity in feed-forward stylization and texture synthesis. In Proceedings of the IEEE Conference on Computer Vision and Pattern Recognition 2017 (pp. 6924–6932).

[25] Liu MY, Tuzel O. Coupled generative adversarial networks. InAdvances in neural information processing systems 2016 (pp. 469–477).

[26] Bousmalis K, Silberman N, Dohan D, Erhan D, Krishnan D. Unsupervised pixel-level domain adaptation with generative adversarial networks. InProceedings of the IEEE conference on computer vision and pattern recognition 2017 (pp. 3722–3731).

[27] Tzeng E, Hoffman J, Darrell T, Saenko K. Simultaneous deep transfer across domains and tasks. InProceedings of the IEEE International Conference on Computer Vision 2015 (pp. 4068–4076).

[28] Ghifary M, Bastiaan Kleijn W, Zhang M, Balduzzi D. Domain generalization for object recognition with multi-task autoencoders. InProceedings of the IEEE international conference on computer vision 2015 (pp. 2551–2559).

[29] Kim T, Cha M, Kim H, Lee JK, Kim J. Learning to discover cross-domain relations with generative adversarial networks. arXiv preprint arXiv:1703.05192. 2017 Mar 15.

[30] Yi Z, Zhang H, Tan P, Gong M. Dualgan: Unsupervised dual learning for image-to-image translation. InProceedings of the IEEE international conference on computer vision 2017 (pp. 2849–2857).

[31] Sohn K, Liu S, Zhong G, Yu X, Yang MH, Chandraker M. Unsupervised domain adaptation for face recognition in unlabeled videos. InProceedings of the IEEE International Conference on Computer Vision 2017 (pp. 3210–3218).

[32] Ren S, He K, Girshick R, Sun J. Faster r-cnn: Towards real-time object detection with region proposal networks. InAdvances in neural information processing systems 2015 (pp. 91–99).

[33] Redmon J, Divvala S, Girshick R, Farhadi A. You only look once: Unified, real-time object detection. InProceedings of the IEEE conference

on computer vision and pattern recognition 2016 (pp. 779–788).

[34] Xu W, He J, Zhang HL, Mao B, Cao J. Real-time target detection and recognition with deep convolutional networks for intelligent visual surveillance. InProceedings of the 9th International Conference on Utility and Cloud Computing 2016 Dec 6 (pp. 321–326).

[35] Chen Y, Li W, Sakaridis C, Dai D, Van Gool L. Domain adaptive faster r-cnn for object detection in the wild. InProceedings of the IEEE conference on computer vision and pattern recognition 2018 (pp. 3339–3348).

[36] Hsu HK, Yao CH, Tsai YH, Hung WC, Tseng HY, Singh M, Yang MH. Progressive domain adaptation for object detection. InThe IEEE Winter Conference on Applications of Computer Vision 2020 (pp. 749–757).

[37] Hoffman J, Wang D, Yu F, Darrell T. Fcns in the wild: Pixel-level adversarial and constraint-based adaptation. arXiv preprint arXiv: 1612.02649. 2016 Dec 8.

[38] Sankaranarayanan S, Balaji Y, Jain A, Nam Lim S, Chellappa R. Learning from synthetic data: Addressing domain shift for semantic segmentation. InProceedings of the IEEE Conference on Computer Vision and Pattern Recognition 2018 (pp. 3752–3761).

[39] Gatys LA, Ecker AS, Bethge M. A neural algorithm of artistic style. arXiv preprint arXiv:1508.06576. 2015 Aug 26.

[40] Li Y, Wang N, Liu J, Hou X. Demystifying neural style transfer. arXiv preprint arXiv:1701.01036. 2017 Jan 4.

[41] Johnson J, Karpathy A, Fei-Fei L. Densecap: Fully convolutional localization networks for dense captioning. InProceedings of the IEEE conference on computer vision and pattern recognition 2016 (pp. 4565–4574).

[42] Chen TH, Liao YH, Chuang CY, Hsu WT, Fu J, Sun M. Show, adapt and tell: Adversarial training of cross-domain image captioner. InProceedings of the IEEE international conference on computer vision 2017 (pp. 521–530).

[43] Zhao W, Xu W, Yang M, Ye J, Zhao Z, Feng Y, Qiao Y. Dual learning for cross-domain image captioning. InProceedings of the 2017 ACM on Conference on Information and Knowledge Management 2017 Nov 6 (pp. 29–38).

[44] Britz D, Le Q, Pryzant R. Effective domain mixing for neural machine translation. InProceedings of the Second Conference on Machine Translation 2017 Sep (pp. 118–126).

[45] Zhang Y, Barzilay R, Jaakkola T. Aspect-augmented adversarial networks for domain adaptation. Transactions of the Association for Computational Linguistics. 2017 Dec;5:515–28.

[46] Yang Z, Hu J, Salakhutdinov R, Cohen WW. Semi-supervised qa with generative domain-adaptive nets. arXiv preprint arXiv:1702.02206. 2017 Feb 7.

[47] Ko WJ, Durrett G, Li JJ. Domain agnostic real-valued specificity prediction. InProceedings of the AAAI Conference on Artificial Intelligence 2019 Jul 17 (Vol. 33, pp. 6610–6617).

[48] Meng Z, Li J, Gaur Y, Gong Y. Domain adaptation via teacher-student learning for end-to-end speech recognition. In2019 IEEE Automatic Speech Recognition and Understanding Workshop (ASRU) 2019 Dec 14 (pp. 268–275). IEEE.

[49] Sun S, Zhang B, Xie L, Zhang Y. An unsupervised deep domain adaptation approach for robust speech recognition. Neurocomputing. 2017 Sep 27;257:79–87.

[50] Denisov P, Vu NT, Font MF. Unsupervised domain adaptation by adversarial learning for robust speech recognition. InSpeech Communication; 13th ITG-Symposium 2018 Oct 10 (pp. 1–5). VDE.

[51] Purushotham S, Carvalho W, Nilanon T, Liu Y. Variational recurrent adversarial deep domain adaptation.

[52] Tonutti M, Ruffaldi E, Cattaneo A, Avizzano CA. Robust and subject-independent driving manoeuvre anticipation through Domain-Adversarial Recurrent Neural Networks. Robotics and Autonomous Systems. 2019 May 1;115:162–73.

[53] Chen C, Miao Y, Lu CX, Xie L, Blunsom P, Markham A, Trigoni N. Motiontransformer: Transferring neural inertial tracking between domains. InProceedings of the AAAI Conference on Artificial Intelligence 2019 Jul 17 (Vol. 33, pp. 8009–8016).

Section 2

Future Trends of Deep Learning

Chapter 4

Deep Learning Enabled Nanophotonics

Lujun Huang, Lei Xu and Andrey E. Miroshnichenko

Abstract

Deep learning has become a vital approach to solving a big-data-driven problem. It has found tremendous applications in computer vision and natural language processing. More recently, deep learning has been widely used in optimising the performance of nanophotonic devices, where the conventional computational approach may require much computation time and significant computation source. In this chapter, we briefly review the recent progress of deep learning in nanophotonics. We overview the applications of the deep learning approach to optimising the various nanophotonic devices. It includes multilayer structures, plasmonic/dielectric metasurfaces and plasmonic chiral metamaterials. Also, nanophotonic can directly serve as an ideal platform to mimic optical neural networks based on nonlinear optical media, which in turn help to achieve high-performance photonic chips that may not be realised based on conventional design method.

Keywords: deep learning, inverse design, plasmonic metasurface, dielectric metasurface, chiral metamaterials, all-optical neural network

1. Introduction

In the past several decades, nanophotonics has been demonstrated as an ideal platform to manipulate the light-matter interaction and engineer the wavefront of the electromagnetic wave at will. The rapid development on nanophotonics has led to tremendous applications ranged from lasing, Lidar, biosensor, LED, photodetector, integrated photonic circuit, invisibility cloak, etc. Nanophotonics covers many exciting topics: photonic crystal, plasmonics, metamaterials, and nanophotonics based on some novel materials (e.g., two-dimensional materials, perovskite). Currently, the building blocks for nanophotonics are made from either metallic or dielectric elements with regular shapes, such as rectangular wire, cylinder, cuboids, and sphere for plasmonic and dielectric metasurfaces. Usually, limited parameters are provided for such a regular structure, and, thus, the optimisation process can be done in a reasonable short time. For example, a single dielectric cylinder with only two parameters, including diameter and height, are involved. Due to the limited freedom, the performance of photonic devices based on the regular pattern is far away from the optimal one. Inverse design method has been widely used to tackle this problem because the full parameter space can be explored [1]. Conventional inverse design methods that include topology optimisation, genetic algorithm, steep descent, and particle swarming optimisation shown in **Figure 1a**, however, require the vast computational source and take a long time to find the optimal

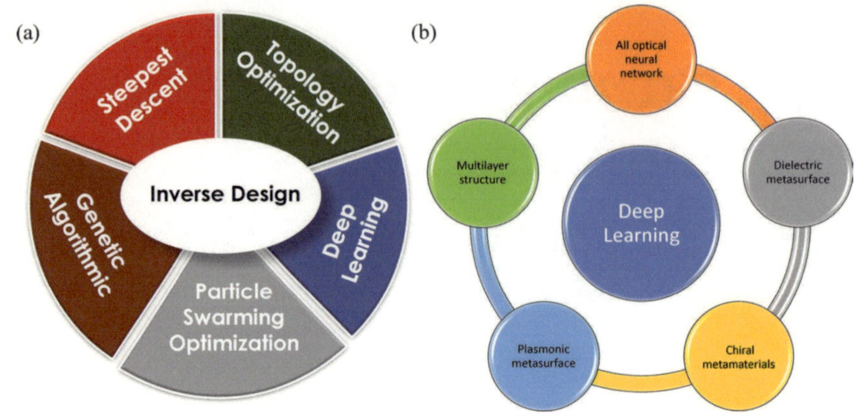

Figure 1.
(a) Inverse design methods in nanophotonics. (b) Application of deep learning in nanophotonics.

local structure. As a branch of machine learning, deep learning has received much attention worldwide because it can efficiently process and analyse a vast number of datasets. It has already found great success in computer vision and speech recognition. Recently, researchers and scientists have applied it to quantum optics, material design and optimisation of nanophotonic devices due to its outstanding capability of finding optimal solution from enormous data. At the same time, the computational cost is much lower compared to other inverse design methods [2, 3]. Several neural networks including deep neural network, generative neural network and convolutional neural network are frequently used to retrieve the optimal structure parameters for irregular structure with limited sets of data and shorter time when many structure parameters are involved for opmisation. This book chapter is organised as follows: In Section 2, we will discuss the inverse design enabled by deep learning on four different topics: multilayer structure, plasmonic metasurface, dielectric metasurface, chiral metamaterials (See **Figure 1b**). In Section 3, we review the recent progress on all-optical neural networks. Then, concluding remarks and outlook are presented in Section 4.

2. Optimisation of nanophotonics design by deep learning

Recently, deep learning using an artificial neural network has emerged as a revolutionary and powerful methodology in nanophotonics field. Applying the deep learning algorithms to the nanophotonic inverse design can introduce remarkable design flexibility which is very challenging and even impossible to achieve based on conventional optimisation approaches [1]. In this section, we will provide a brief review of the implementation of deep learning to solve nanophotonic inverse design problems.

2.1 Design of multilayer nanostructures by deep learning

Multilayer nanostructures can exhibit unique optical properties including field enhancements and distributions, special transmission/reflection spectra, based on the interference of different modes supported by different layers in the nanostructures. Machine learning has emerged as a more and more promising tool to solve the inverse design of photonic nanostructures. It will enable effective inverse design by simultaneously considering various inter-linked parameters such as geometric parameters, material types, etc., simultaneously (unlike the current regular approaches, which optimise one or two parameters only, at a time).

A recent work done by Peurifoy et al. has demonstrated using deep neural network (DNN) to relate the geometry of SiO_2/TiO_2 multilayer spherical core-shell nanoparticles with their light-scattering properties (**Figure 2a**) [4]. The transfer matrix method has been used to analytically solve the scatterings to generate 50,000 different combinations of the shell thickness as the total examples for training, validation, and testing. The forward learning model was a fully-connected dense feed-forward network with four hidden layers. The inputs were set to be the thickness of each shell of the nanoparticles, and the outputs were the corresponding scattering cross section spectra. During the learning process, the output of the network was compared with the target response to provide a loss function against which the weights can be trained and updated. After the forward-feeding training process, by fixing the weights, and setting the inputs as a trainable variable and fix the output to the desired output, they run the neural network backwardly, let the neural networks to iterate the inputs and provide the desired geometry to give the target spectrum. After training, as can be seen from **Figure 2a**, for an arbitrarily given spectrum (blue curve), the DNN can successfully predict the thickness of each shell of the nanoparticles that can generate a similar scattering spectrum as wanted, with some minor deviations.

A further improvement of this approach is to take into account the different material combinations for the core-shell nanoparticles. In another work done by So et al., they have considered a simultaneous inverse design of materials and structural parameters using the deep learning network (**Figure 2b**) [5]. Here, they use the network to map the extinction spectra of the electric dipole (ED) and magnetic dipole (MD) to the core-shell nanoparticles, including the material information and shell thicknesses. The DL model consists of two networks: a designed network to learn a mapping from optical properties to design parameters, and a spectrum network to learn from design parameters to optical properties. Here, in order to adapt the network to the different types of input data (materials and thicknesses), the loss function has been devised accordingly by the weighted average of material

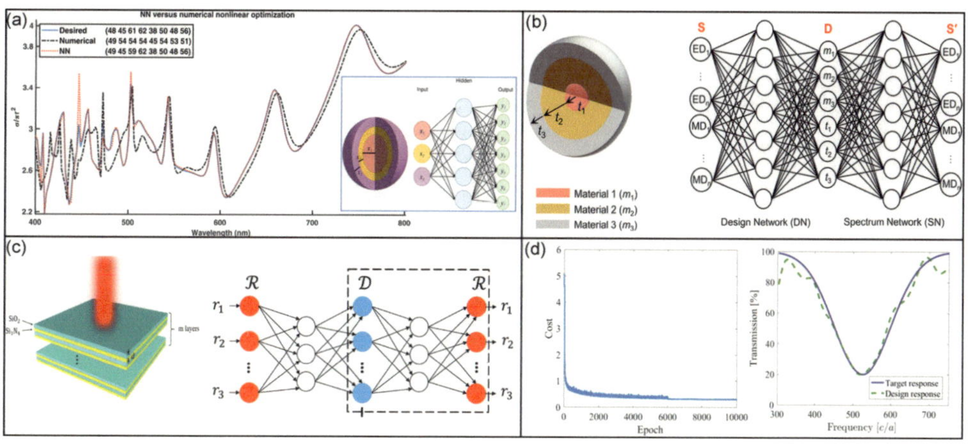

Figure 2.
Application of DL for multilayer nanostructure design: (a) using DNN to retrieve the layer thicknesses of a multilayer particle based on its scattering spectrum. Inset: Network architecture. (b) Left: Geometry of three-layered core-shell nanoparticles with changeable materials and thicknesses. Right: Network architecture. (c) Left: Multilayer thin films of SiO_2 and Si_3N_4. Right: The architecture of the tandem network composed of an inverse design network and a forward modelling network. (d) Left: Evolution of the training cost of the network. Right: Performance of the network using a Gaussian-shaped spectrum.

and structural losses: $l_{\text{design}} = \rho l_{\text{structure}} + (1-\rho) l_{\text{material}}$ with ρ the weight of the structural error, which is also set as a hyper-parameter to be adjusted during the training process. The loss $l_{\text{structure}}$ was evaluated by the mean absolute error $l_{\text{MSE}}(x,y) = \frac{1}{n}\sum_n (x_n - y_n)^2$, while the loss function for the materials l_{material} was evaluated by binary cross-entropy with logits loss $l_{\text{BCE}}(x,y) = -[y log\sigma(x) + (1-y)\log(1-\sigma(x))]$, with x and y being the target and output, respectively, and $\sigma(x)$ is the Sigmoid function. After training, the network has demonstrated great ability to realise the inverse design for different types of problems, including spectral tuning the electric or magnetic resonances, or overlapping them which potentially facilitate the inverse design of nanostructures with specific functions, such as zero-forward (first Kerker condition) or zero-backwards (second Kerker condition) scatterings [6, 7].

A similar network has also been used to explore the optical transmission spectra from multilayer thin films (**Figure 2c, d**) [8]. Here, Liu et al. combined the forward network modelling and inverse design in tandem architecture to overcome the data inconsistency which originates from the non-uniqueness in inverse scattering problems, i.e., the same optical responses can correspond to different designs. This non-uniqueness of the response-to-design mapping will cause conflicting examples within the training set and might lead to non-convergence of the neural network. The TN architecture consists of an inverse-design network connected to a forward model network. The forward network learns the mapping from the structural parameters to the optical responses and is trained separately first. After the forward network is trained, it is placed after the inverse-design model network, and its network weights remain fixed during the training of the inverse-design model network. The inverse-design network learns a mapping from the optical responses to the structural parameters. After the training process, such a DNN can efficiently predict the geometry of a device which is both promising and much faster as compared with the conventional electromagnetic solvers. As shown in the right diagram of **Figure 2d**, the learning curve of this tandem neural network has demonstrated a fast convergence during the training process. The structures designed by the network matches the desired transmission spectra with high fidelity.

2.2 Design of plasmonic metasurfaces by deep learning

Plasmonic metasurfaces have become the building blocks for the meta-optics field. It allows for manipulating the wavefront of the electromagnetic wave at will. In this section, we are going to give a summary of the current status applying deep learning approach for inversely designing plasmonic metasurfaces.

In recent years, with the burgeoning field of metasurfaces, deep learning has emerged as a powerful tool for realising efficient inverse design of different types of plasmonic metasurfaces for different applications including spectral control, near-field design [9–11]. In 2018, Malkiel et al. introduced a novel bidirectional DNN model which can realise both the design and characterisation of plasmonic metasurfaces [12]. The network consists of two standard DNNs: a geometry-predicting network (GPN) to solve the inverse design and a spectrum-predicting network (SPN) to solve the spectra prediction tasks for plasmonic metasurfaces of "H"-shaped gold nanostructures. They have shown that by combing these two networks and optimise them together, they can co-adapt to each other, which is more effective than training them separately, as shown in **Figure 3a**. The training data for the GPN consists of three groups of data: desired spectra for x-polarised pump and y-polarised pump, and the materials' properties. Each group of data is fed into a different layer and three DNNs in parallel before they join the fully connected joint

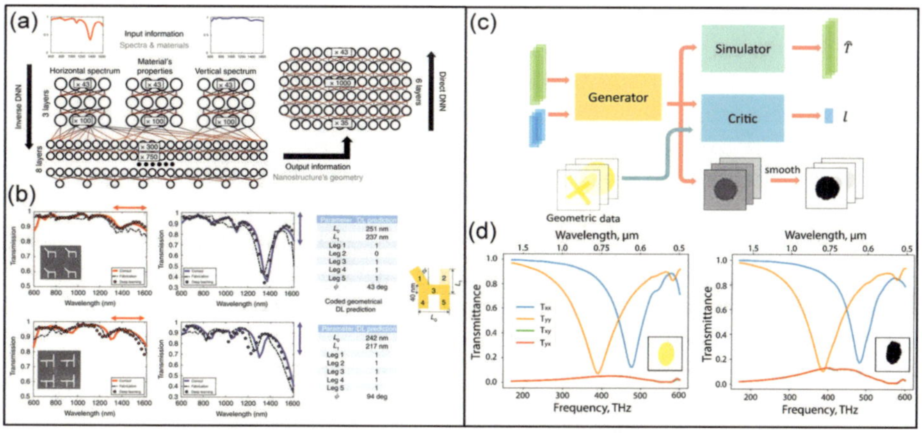

Figure 3.
Application of DL for plasmonic metasurfaces inverse design: (a) architecture of the DNN composed of xxx. (b) Demonstration of the inverse design of "H"-shaped gold metasurfaces. (c) The architecture of a proposed GAN model composed of a generator, a simulator, and a critic. (d) Transmission spectra of the original (left) and generated (right) patterns from the proposed GAN approach.

layers. This architecture has considered the differences of properties in the inputs' data, thus allows a better performance of the networks suitable for the nanophotonic design. After that, they were using the predicted geometry from the GPN to feed the SPN and returns the predicted transmission spectra as the outputs. Then the back-propagation is used to optimise both networks. The networks show excellent agreement between the measurements, predictions and simulations, as demonstrated by two examples shown in **Figure 3b** using the network to realise the inverse design of "H"-shaped gold metasurfaces for target spectra.

As the structural complexity grows, the generation of the training data sets takes enormous time. Furthermore, the requirement for more degrees of freedom in metasurface patterns makes the problems more and more challenging for conventional neural networks. To solve this issue, generative adversarial network (GAN) has been employed for metasurface designs recently [13]. A GAN involves placing two neural networks (a generator and a critic) in competition with each other and trying to reach an optimum, as shown in **Figure 3c**. Here, the simulator was first pretrained using 6500 full-wave finite element method (FEM) simulations for metasurfaces with different shapes. After the training, the simulator was used to approximate the transmission spectra of any input patterns rather than using the full-wave FEM simulations to do it. This has significantly reduced the number of datasets for the network. The generator is used to produce the metasurface patterns in response to a given input spectra T, and then fed into the simulator to get the approximated spectra T′. The critic will compare the original input geometric data corresponding to T and the generated patterns from the generator and guide the generator to produce patterns that share common features with the geometric input data. **Figure 3d** gives one example demonstrating the excellent performance of this network on predicting and identifying the structure to produce the target spectra with only minor deviations.

2.3 Design of dielectric metasurface by deep learning

Recently, dielectric metasurface has triggered extensive interests in the past decades. Analogous to metallic nanostructures supporting plasmonic resonance, high index dielectric nanostructures provide multipole electric and magnetic resonance (also called as Mie resonance), which enable 2π phase coverage without ease. Besides, the intrinsic material loss is much lower for high index semiconductor than the counterpart of noble metals. These two unique properties make it possible to develop high-performance photonic devices based on dielectric metasurface. Although dielectric metasurfaces with such regular elements have much better performance compared to the plasmonic metasurfaces, they still do not reach the optimal one with the best efficiency. In order to further improve the performance of dielectric metasurface, inverse design approaches, including adjoint-based topology optimisation and genetic algorithms, have been widely used. The iterative optimisation methods lead to the findings of devices with high efficiency with irregular patterns which are usually beyond human intuition. However, these methods rely on extremely heavy computation, making them hard to apply to sophisticated devices featured by a very high dimensional design space. The recently developed deep learning approach, which is based on artificial neural networks, is viewed as the perfect solution of dealing massive data while reducing the computation cost. It has already found great success in computer vision and natural language processing. Recently, researchers have transferred deep learning to the inverse design of nanophotonic devices. Up to date, most frequently used neural networks in the design of dielectric metasurfaces are DNN, GAN, and convolution neural networks (CNN) In the following, we will illustrate them one by one and also discuss their unique strengths and drawbacks.

DNN with fully connected layers has been demonstrated as a versatile and efficient way of engineering a high-Q resonance with desired characteristics, including linewidth, amplitude, and spectral location [14]. The structure considered here is double identical silicon nanobars sitting on the substrate, as shown in **Figure 4b**. The width and length of nanobars are,, respectively, denoted as W and L while the centre to centre distance between nanobars is denoted as $2x_0$. To reduce the structure complexity, the period of the unit cell and the thickness of silicon bars are fixed as p = 900 nm and t = 150 nm, respectively. Previous studies have demonstrated that

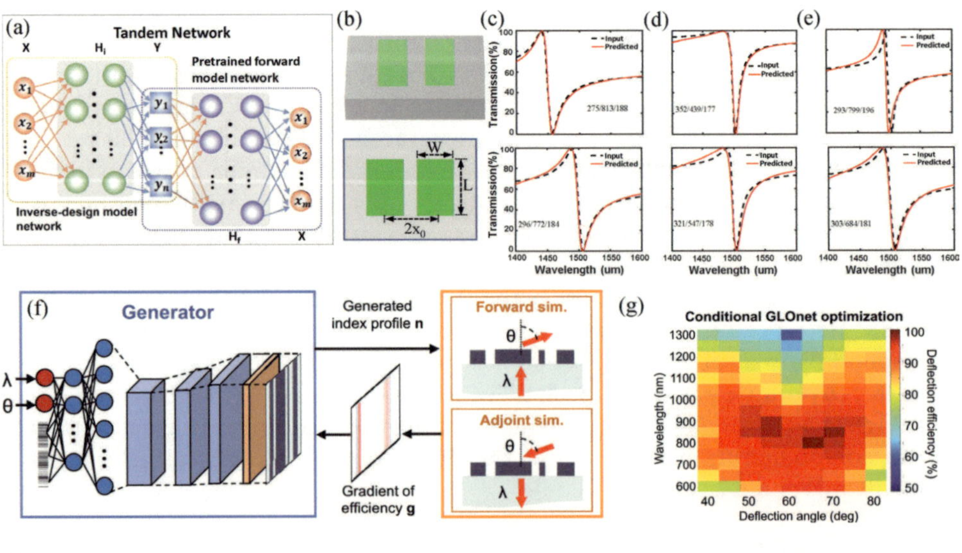

Figure 4.
(a) The architecture of the tandem network, which consists of inverse-design model network followed by the pretrained forward mode network. (b) Schematic drawing of the unit cell made of two identical silicon nanobar. Inverse design of metasurface supporting Fano profile spectra (c) λ_0 = 1450 nm and 1500 nm, $\Delta\lambda$ = 15 nm, q = 0.8. (d) λo = 1500 nm, $\Delta\lambda$ = 10 nm, q = 0.3 and q = 0.5. (e) λ_0 = 1500 nm, $\Delta\lambda$ = 5 nm and $\Delta\lambda$ = 15 nm, q = 0.7. (f) Schematic of the conditional GLOnet for metagrating design. (g) Optimised efficiency of metagrating from the conditional GLOnet.

such an array structure support a Fano resonance induced by the quasi bound state in the continuum. Since there are three parameters to be tuned, it is very challenging to find the desired structure parameters by one by one brute-force searching when the spectrum response is predefined. DNN can correctly address this issue in an reduced time period. 25,000 sets of the training data are randomly generated with rigorous coupled-wave analysis (RCWA). It is worth noting that it is straightforward and easy to train the network mapping from structure parameters to reflection/ transmission spectrum because one set of structure parameters can only produce a given spectrum. The objective is to search the structure parameter for the desired spectra response. It might be challenging to use an only forward neural network to find out the required parameters because the non-uniqueness issue arises. In other words, different designs may produce the same far-field electromagnetic response because the optical resonance is mainly governed by the volume of structure but shows weak dependence on the structure shape. To solve this one-to-many issue, as shown in **Figure 4a**, a Tandem neural network consisting of inverse design model network and the forward model network is proposed. More specifically, the forward network is trained first to learn the mapping from structure parameters to the optical response. After the training of the forward network is done, inverse design model network is trained while the weight and bias for the forward network are fixed. Once the full training process is completed, one can retrieve the structure parameters in several milliseconds while the optical spectrum is predefined. In order to test the validity of Tandem network, **Figure 4c–e** compares the predefined spectrum and predicted spectrum of Fano resonance with different wavelength, linewidth and amplitude. The excellent agreement can be found between two, indicating the effectiveness of the deep learning approach in the inverse design of nanophotonics. Note that only amplitude of transmission spectrum is considered here. In many applications of dielectric metasurface (e.g., metalens), both amplitude and phase should be considered to shape the wavefront of electromagnetic wave. Since optical resonance is always accompanied by π phase-shift, which may make training difficult for phase spectra because it is better to be differentiated for output parameters (i.e., phase or amplitude). Instead of using phase and amplitude, researchers adopt both real and imaginary parts of the reflection/transmission spectrum as the output of training data.

Moreover, because of the huge mismatch between the dimensions of input and output, a revised neural network was applied. The first standard linear neural network was replaced with the bilinear tensor layer that can correlate two entity vectors in multiple dimensions. Training results indicated that modified neural network converges faster than the standard linear neural network. This is because input parameters are interdependent on each other. Taking an array of dielectric nanodisk as an example, the structure is fully described by four parameters: refractive index of materials, radius and height of disk, the gap between disks. As we mentioned previously, the optical resonance is mainly determined by the refractive index and volume of structures. In other words, the spectrum response is governed by permittivity ($\varepsilon = n^2$) and volume ($V = \pi r^2 h$). Therefore, multiplication of two entities by bilinear tensor can better describe the nonlinearity, and thus facilitate the training process. However, it is worth pointing out that there are some limitations on deep neural network. First, the design solution retrieved from deep learning must fall into the boundary of the training data set. Second, it only works for structure defined by several simple parameters. When more parameters are involved, tens, hundreds of thousands of training data are required to guarantee the prediction accuracy. As a consequence, generating such a large amount of data may consume a long time and cause a high computational cost. Moreover, it will be challenging to train the data for dielectric metasurface with free form geometry via DNN.

GAN has been found to overcome the above limitations effectively. GAN is originally proposed in the computer vision. It is capable of creating artificial images that even cannot be distinguished from true images by the computers [15]. GAN has been successfully applied to the design of subwavelength scale metallic nanostructures and multifunctional dielectric metasurface [13, 16]. The operation principles of GAN in the design of metasurface are described as follows. The unit cell of the metasurface is divided into N*N (i.e., N = 32, 64) pixel images while the thickness of structure and period of the unit cell is fixed. There are two neural networks in GAN: generator and discriminator. The generator networks try to create the image so that it cannot be differentiated to the real image. In contrast, the discriminator networks are trained to distinguish the image produced by the generator from the real image sets. The competing process between these two networks leads to the creation of artificial images that cannot be distinguished from the real one. In fact, the topology optimisation method or deep learning approach does not always work alone. They can be combined together to build up a new generative network. Such a generative network has been proposed to optimise the efficiency of metagrating at large angle across a broadband wavelength range because it took both the advantages of GAN and adjoint-based topology optimisation [17]. Although GAN requires less training sets, the training data may be optimised first and thus demand more computation source. More recently, global topology optimisation networks (GLOnets) was proposed by Jiang et al. from Stanford [18, 19]. It incorporates the adjoint-based optimisation into the generative neural networks. Unlike DNN and GAN methods, it does not require pre-calculation of training data based on the electromagnetic solver. Instead, it adopts the generator networks followed by the adjoint-based topology optimiser, allowing for direct learning the physical relationship between geometry parameters of the device and electromagnetic response, as shown in **Figure 4f**. Such a global optimiser does not only reduce the computation time but also further improve the efficiency of metagrating at large angles compared to the topology optimisation method (See **Figure 4g**).

2.4 Design of chiral metamaterials by deep learning

Another example of deep learning's application in nanophotonics is to design plasmonic chiral metamaterials [20, 21]. Chirality corresponds to the structure–property of an object which cannot superpose to its mirror image by any combination of rotation and translation. It shows different response under the illumination of left circular polarisation (LCP) and right circular polarisation (RCP) incidence. This concept is originated from molecules or ions in chemistry. However, the optical chirality in nature is extremely weak due to the small interaction volume in the visible wavelength. The emergence of metamaterials makes it possible to realise a strong optical chiral response. It is well established that a pair of rotating gold split-ring resonators (SRRs) separated by a dielectric spacer can induce strong chirality. The question of how to optimise the chirality at the given frequency still remain unanswered because so many parameters involved make it difficult to find out the optimal design [20]. The advent of machine learning approach provided the possibility of processing many parameters at once in a reasonable short time. Ma et al. developed a deep learning-based model to design and optimise three-dimensional plasmonic chiral metamaterials at the desired wavelength. The structure they considered is shown in **Figure 5a**. The period of the unit cell is fixed as 2.5 μm while the thickness and width of gold SRR are set as 200 nm and 50 nm, respectively. Other parameters, such as length of top and bottom SRR ($l1$ and l_2), top and bottom dielectric space layer (t_1 and t_2), and the twisted angle α between two SRRs, are set as input parameters. For output parameters, 201 points are sampled in the reflection

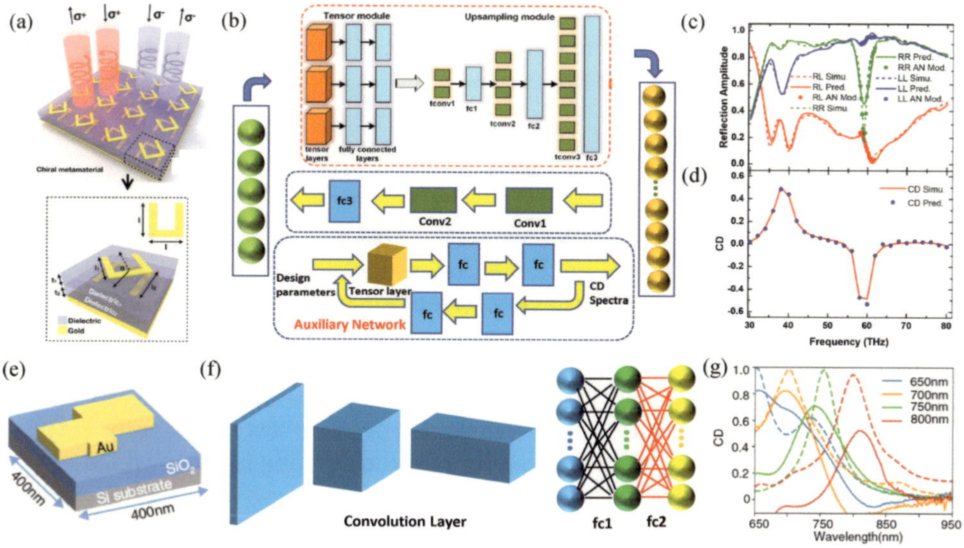

Figure 5.
(a) Schematic drawing of unit cell for chiral metamaterials. (b) Architecture of neural network used for the inverse design of chiral metamaterials. (c) Reflection spectra calculated from numerical simulation and predicted from DNN. (d) Chirality spectra for both numerical simulation and DNN prediction. (e) Schematic drawing of unit cells of structure used for inverse design. (f) Schematic of BoNet for optimisation of the far-field spectrum. (g) BoNet predicted and experimental verification of far-field circular dichroism spectra at the desired wavelength of 650, 700, 750 and 800 nm.

spectrum from 30 to 80 THz. Here, four characteristic reflection spectra that include R_{LL} (LCP-input: LCP-output), R_{LR} (LCP-input: LCP-output), R_{RR} (RCP-input: RCP-output) and chirality spectrum are investigated as output parameters. **Figure 5b** shows the structure of DNN that consists of primary networks (PN) and auxiliary network (AN). Both networks have a forward path and an inverse path. For the forward path of PN, the huge mismatch of dimension between input parameters (1 × 5) and output parameters (3 × 201) makes it hard to converge. This is especially obvious around the resonant frequency. To avoid this issue, a neural tensor network followed by the unsampled module is used. Instead of using DNN with fully connected layers that are formed by simply linear recombination from previous neurons, the first hidden layer is replaced as the neural tensor network to model second-order relationships because the input parameters are not independent with each other. **Figure 5c** compares the reflection spectra obtained from electromagnetic simulation and prediction of PN. The excellent agreement can be found for most wavelengths except around resonant wavelengths. This issue is well addressed by introducing another AN which learns the relationship between structural parameters and chirality spectrum. The results are shown in **Figure 5d**. After finishing the training both PN and AN, one can construct any chirality spectrum feature by single or double resonances as well as optimise the chirality at predefined spectrum. Note that such networks are not the only one which can design and optimise the chiral metamaterials. Li et al. developed a self-consistent framework termed BoNet (Bayesian optimisation (BO) and CNN) [21], which can conduct self-learning on the optical properties of nanostructure (i.e., near field and far-field). The unit cell of structure, as shown in **Figure 5e**, is divided into 40 × 40 pixels, where the empty area is denoted as 0, and the gold brick area is denoted as 1. Other parameters, such as period and thickness, are fixed. DNN used here is composed of convolution layers followed by several fully connected layers (see **Figure 5f**). Successful training on the BoNet can help to optimise the chirality at an arbitrary wavelength in the visible wavelength range. **Figure 5g** shows the chirality spectra of measurement and prediction from BoNet. The discrepancy can be attributed to the tolerance of fabrication and measurements.

3. All-optical neural networks

As was discussed above, neural networks have been successfully used to solve rather complex problems in nanophotonics in particular. There are two fundamentally different alternatives for the implementation of neural networks: a software simulation in conventional computers or a particular hardware solution capable of dramatically decreasing execution time. Software simulation can be useful to develop and debug new algorithms, as well as to benchmark them using small networks. However, if large networks are to be used, software simulation is not enough. The problem is the time required for the learning process, which can increase exponentially with the size of the network.

At the same time, there are ongoing attempts to implement this architecture in a hardware form, which should allow for substantial gains for scaling and distributed approaches. Digital circuits are usually implemented by using robust CMOS technology, where the neuron state summation is realised via common multipliers and adders. The activation function is more complicated to implement, which require a highly nonlinear response. One of the technical difficulties is related to the implementation of communication channels. In general, the connection scales as a square of the number of inputs. One of the solutions to this problem can be provided by optical networks, where the communication channels do not need to be hard-wired [22, 23]. Also, in free space, light waves can cross each other without affecting the carrying information. Other benefits include low energy to transmit the signal and high switching time up to 40 GHz. Thus, analogue optical technology allows to implement artificial neural networks directly in hardware, with data encoded in pulses of light and neurons made from optical elements, such as lenses, prisms, beam splitters, waveguides and spatial light modulators (SLMs), see **Figure 6a**. In particular, SLMs are used for algebraic operations, including matrix multiplication with a specific phase mask design [24].

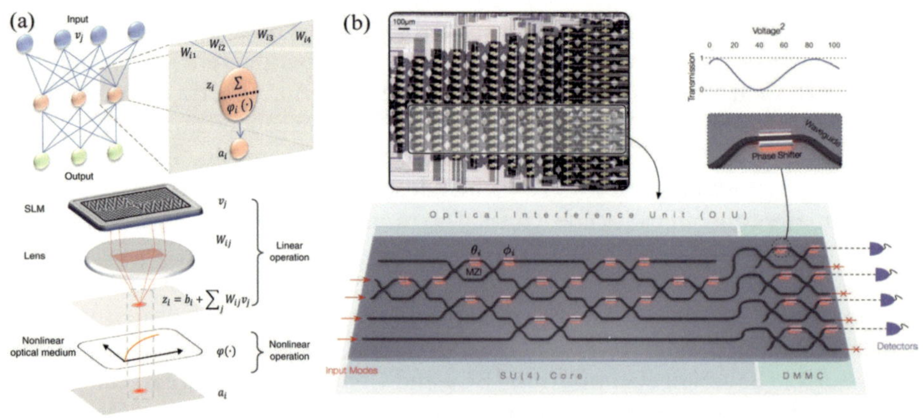

Figure 6.
(a) Schematic of a generic two-layer artificial optical neural network with linear operation realised via programmable SLM and nonlinear activation by employing nonlinear media. (b) Optical micrograph and highlighted region of the implemented optical neural network of 22-mode on-chip interference unit. The system acts as an optical FPGA. Matrix multiplication and amplification are realised fully optically via Mach-Zehnder interferometer (MZI) phase-shifters.

Recently, another approach to realise optical neural networks was based on Mach-Zehnder interferometers (MZIs) to calculate matrix products [25, 26], see **Figure 6b**. By carefully manipulating a specific phase shift between a coherent pair of incoming light pulses allow to multiply a two-element vector, encoded in the amplitude of the pulses, by a two-by-two matrix [27, 28]. An array of the interferometers can then perform arbitrary matrix operations, which is widely used, for example, in the boson sampling approach.

One of the main challenges for the successful realisation of the optical neural networks is to find a suitable implementation of the activation function. Due to its inherent nonlinear response, light pulses are required to interact with a nonlinear media. Various nonlinear effects have been proposed for such functionality. To avoid optical signal loss, mostly dielectric materials have been considered. It includes photorefractive crystals, liquid crystals, and various semiconductors [29]. Most promising nonlinear effects are based on harmonics generation, phase conjugation, optical limiter, and bistable response. Recently, researchers from The Hong Kong University of Science and Technology proposed a new approach based on cold atoms exhibiting electromagnetic induced transparency effect to implement the nonlinear activation function [24]. Importantly, it requires very weak laser power and is based on nonlinear quantum interference. It is also possible to produce different activation functions by varying the positions of counterpropagating beams.

The group from the University of Münster has suggested an alternative approach by exploiting the wavelength-division multiplexing (WDM) to transport and sum multiple pulses at different wavelengths using single waveguides [30]. Importantly, they suggest a phase-change material (PCM) for both linear summing and nonlinear firing. In this approach, each neuron is implemented as a ring-shaped resonator of varying diameters to tap light signals with corresponding resonant wavelengths from a common waveguide. When the total power of all those signals exceeds a certain threshold, they then switch another piece of PCM, this time embedded in a resonator at the neuron's output.

Despite recent progress in all-optical implementation of neural networks, various groups investigated hybrid optoelectronic systems in which neurons convert signals from light into electricity and then back to light. The group from Princeton suggested using electro-absorption modulation for the optimal integrated photonics implementation of the neural networks [31]. One of the essential aspects is the integration density. The electro-optical induced nonlinearity is realised by using photodiode couplers. Moreover, it also allows for spiking signal processing, which enables the direct implementation of neuromorphic computing. It led to the development of a new and quite promising platform of neuromorphic photonics combining the advantages of optics and electronics to build systems with high efficiency, high interconnectivity and high information density.

4. Conclusion and outlook

Although deep learning was proposed and found great success in the context of computer vision and speech/image recognition, it has become a powerful approach to solve complex problems in biology, physics and chemistry. As a branch of physics, nanophotonics has witnessed huge progress based on deep learning. Deep learning allows us to inversely design nanophotonic devices with even less computation source and time compared to conventional computational approaches, such as topology optimisation and genetic algorithm. Currently, the research interests and efforts are still fast-growing and expanding in deep learning-enabled nanophotonics. More research opportunities may be brought in this area.

On the one hand, although deep learning has been successfully applied to retrieve the structure parameters for any given spectrum, it remains an opening question that whether it is possible to realise narrowband or broadband absorbers at the specified wavelength or wavelength range. On the other hand, by combining deep learning and topology optimisation, beam steering at relatively large deflection angle with high efficiency has been demonstrated for single- or bi-operation wavelengths. Next step is to utilise deep learning to optimise the metasurface design with multi-functionalities further. For example, current broadband achromatic metalens has limited focusing efficiency. We believe the deep learning can entirely overcome this limitation by providing more irregular combinations of metaatoms that cannot be found by regular cylinder metaatoms. Finally, since nanophotonics offers a powerful and versatile platform to realise optical neural networks, more advanced and fast photonic chips that can bypass the computational capability based on traditional electric chips will be developed and paved the way toward the photonic computer.

Acknowledgements

The authors acknowledge the funding support provided by UNSW Scientia Fellowship and ARC Discovery Project (DP170103778).

Conflict of interest

The authors declare no conflict of interest.

Author details

Lujun Huang[1], Lei Xu[1,2] and Andrey E. Miroshnichenko[1]*

1 School of Engineering and Information Technology, University of New South Wales, Canberra, Australia

2 Advanced Optics and Photonics Laboratory, Department of Engineering, School of Science & Technology, Nottingham Trent University, Nottingham, United Kingdom

*Address all correspondence to: andrey.miroshnichenko@unsw.edu.au

References

[1] Molesky S, Lin Z, Piggott A, Jin W, Vuckovic J, Rodriguez A. Inverse design in nanophotonics. Nature Photonics. 2018;**12**:659-670. DOI: 10.1038/s41566-018-0246-9

[2] Yao K, Unni R, Zheng Y. Intelligent nanophotonics: Merging photonics and artificial intelligence at the nanoscale. Nano. 2019;**8**:339-366. DOI: 10.1515/nanoph-2018-0183

[3] Zhang Q, Yu H, Barbiero M, Wang B, Gu M. Artificial neural networks enabled by nanophotonics. Light: Science and Applications. 2019;**8**:42. DOI: 10.1038/s41377-019-0151-0

[4] Peurifoy J, Shen Y, Jing L, Yang Y, Cano-Renteria F, Delacy B, et al. Nanophotonic particle simulation and inverse design using artificial neural networks. Science Advances. 2018;**4**:1-8. DOI: 10.1126/sciadv.aar4206

[5] So S, Mun J, Rho J. Simultaneous inverse design of materials and structures via deep learning: Demonstration of dipole resonance engineering using core–shell nanoparticles. ACS Applied Materials & Interfaces. 2019;**11**:24264-24268. DOI: 10.1021/acsami.9b05857

[6] Fu Y, Kuznetsov A, Miroshnichenko A, Yu Y, Luk'yanchuk B. Directional visible light scattering by silicon nanoparticles. Nature Communications. 2013;**4**:1527. DOI: 10.1038/ncomms2538

[7] Paniagua-Domínguez R, Yu Y, Miroshnichenko A, Krivitsky L, Fu Y, Valuckas V, et al. Generalized brewster effect in dielectric metasurfaces. Nature Communications. 2016;**7**:10362. DOI: 10.1038/ncomms10362

[8] Liu D, Tan Y, Khoram E, Yu Z. Training deep neural networks for the inverse design of nanophotonic structures. ACS Photonics. 2018;**5**:1365-1369. DOI: 10.1021/acsphotonics.7b01377

[9] Baxter J, Lesina A, Guay J, Weck A, Berini P, Ramunno L. Plasmonic colours predicted by deep learning. Scientific Reports. 2019;**9**:8074. DOI: 10.1038/s41598-019-44522-7

[10] He J, He C, Zheng C, Wang Q, Ye J. Plasmonic nanoparticle simulations and inverse design using machine learning. Nanoscale. 2019;**11**:17444-17459. DOI: 10.1039/C9NR03450A

[11] Lin R, Zhai Y, Xiong C, Li X. Inverse design of plasmonic metasurfaces by convolutional neural network. Optics Letters. 2020;**45**:1362. DOI: 10.1364/OL.387404

[12] Malkiel I, Mrejen M, Nagler A, Arieli U, Wolf L, Suchowski H. Plasmonic nanostructure design and characterisation via deep learning. Light: Science and Applications. 2018;**7**:60. DOI: 10.1038/s41377-018-0060-7

[13] Liu Z, Zhu D, Rodrigues S, Lee K, Cai W. Generative model for the inverse design of metasurfaces. Nano Letters. 2018;**18**:6570-6576. DOI: 10.1021/acs.nanolett.8b03171

[14] Xu L, Rahmani M, Smirnova D, Kamali K, Deng F, Chiang Y, et al. Enhanced light–matter interactions in dielectric nanostructures via machine-learning approach. Advanced Photonics. 2020;**2**:026003. DOI: 10.1117/1.AP.2.2.026003

[15] An S, Fowler C, Zheng B, Shalaginov M, Tang H, Li H, et al. A deep learning approach for objective-driven all-dielectric metasurface design. ACS Photonics. 2019;**6**:3196-3207. DOI: 10.1021/acsphotonics.9b00966

[16] Goodfellow I, Pouget-Abadie J, Mirza M, Xu B, Warde-Farley D, Ozair S, et al. Generative adversarial nets. In: Proceedings of the International Conference on Neural Information Processing Systems (NIPS 2014); Montréal, Canada; 8-13 December, 2014. pp. 2672-2680

[17] An S, Zheng B, Tang H, Shalaginov M, Zhou L, Li H, et al. Generative Multi-Functional Meta-Atom and Metasurface Design Networks. arXiv:1908.04851

[18] Jiang J, Sell D, Hoyer S, Hickey J, Yang J, Fan J. Free-form diffractive metagrating design based on generative adversarial networks. ACS Nano. 2019;**13**:8872-8878. DOI: 10.1021/acsnano.9b02371

[19] Jiang J, Fan J. Global optimisation of dielectric metasurfaces using a physics-driven neural network. Nano Letters. 2019;**19**:5366-5372. DOI: 10.1021/acs.nanolett.9b01857

[20] Jiang J, Fan J. Simulator-based training of generative neural networks for the inverse design of metasurfaces. Nanophotonics. 2020;**9**:1059-1069. DOI: 10.1515/nanoph-2019-0330

[21] Ma W, Cheng F, Liu Y. Deep-learning-enabled on-demand design of chiral metamaterials. ACS Nano. 2018;**12**:6326-6334. DOI: 10.1021/acsnano.8b03569

[22] Li Y, Xu Y, Jiang M, Li B, Han T, Chi C, et al. Generative model for the inverse design of metasurfaces. Physical Review Letters. 2019;**123**:213902. DOI: 10.1103/PhysRevLett.123.213902

[23] Sui X, Wu Q, Liu J, Chen Q, Gu G. A review of optical neural networks. IEEE Access. 2020;**8**:70773-70783. DOI: 10.1109/ACCESS.2020.2987333

[24] Zuo Y, Li B, Zhao Y, Jiang Y, Chen Y, Chen P, et al. All-optical neural network with nonlinear activation functions. Optica. 2019;**6**:1132-1137. DOI: 10.1364/OPTICA.6.001132

[25] Shen Y, Harris N, Skirlo S, Prabhu M, Baehhr-Jones T, Hochberg M, et al. Deep Learning with Coherent Nanophotonic Circuits. 2016. arXiv:1610.02365

[26] Hughes T, Minkov M, Shi Y, Fan S. Training of photonic neural networks through in situ backpropagation and gradient measurement. Optica. 2018;**5**:864-871. DOI: 10.1364/OPTICA.5.000864

[27] Zhang T, Wang J, Dan Y, Lanqiu Y, Dai J, Han X, et al. Efficient training and design of photonic neural network through neuroevolution. Optics Express. 2018;**27**:37150-37163. DOI: 10.1364/OE.27.037150

[28] George J, Mehrabian A, Amin R, Meng J, Lima T, Tait A, et al. Neuromorphic photonics with electro-absorption modulators. Optics Express. 2019;**27**:5181-5191. DOI: 10.1364/OE.27.005181

[29] Denz C. Optical Neural Networks. New York: Springer; 1998. DOI: 10.1007/978-3-663-12272-2

[30] Feldmann J, Youngblood N, Wright C, Bhaskaran, Pernice W. All-optical spiking neurosynaptic networks with self-learning capabilities. Nature. 2019;**569**:208-214. DOI: 10.1038/s41586-019-1157-8

[31] Tait A, Lima T, Nahmias M, Miller H, Peng H, Shastri B, et al. Silicon photonic modulator neuron. Physical Review Applied. 2019;**11**:064043. DOI: 10.1103/PhysRevApplied.11.064043

Chapter 5

Explainable Artificial Intelligence (xAI) Approaches and Deep Meta-Learning Models

Evren Dağlarli

Abstract

The explainable artificial intelligence (xAI) is one of the interesting issues that has emerged recently. Many researchers are trying to deal with the subject with different dimensions and interesting results that have come out. However, we are still at the beginning of the way to understand these types of models. The forthcoming years are expected to be years in which the openness of deep learning models is discussed. In classical artificial intelligence approaches, we frequently encounter deep learning methods available today. These deep learning methods can yield highly effective results according to the data set size, data set quality, the methods used in feature extraction, the hyper parameter set used in deep learning models, the activation functions, and the optimization algorithms. However, there are important shortcomings that current deep learning models are currently inadequate. These artificial neural network-based models are black box models that generalize the data transmitted to it and learn from the data. Therefore, the relational link between input and output is not observable. This is an important open point in artificial neural networks and deep learning models. For these reasons, it is necessary to make serious efforts on the explainability and interpretability of black box models.

Keywords: explainable artificial intelligence (xAI), meta-learning, deep learning

1. Introduction

Explainable artificial intelligence (xAI) is one of the research topics that has been intriguing in recent years. Today, even if we are at the beginning of understanding this type of models, the studies that show interesting results about this issue are getting more and more intensive. In the near future, it is predicted that there will be years when the interpretability of artificial intelligence and deep meta-learning models is frequently explored [1]. It is thought to be a solution to overcome constraints in classical deep learning methods.

In classical artificial intelligence approaches, we frequently encounter deep learning methods available today. Currently, in classical deep learning methods, input data and target (class) information can be trained with high performance and tested with new data input [2]. These deep learning methods can yield highly effective results according to the data set size, data set quality, the methods used in feature extraction, the hyper parameter set used in deep learning models, the activation functions, and the optimization algorithms [3]. Many layers in a deep network allow it to recognize things at different levels of abstraction. For example, in a structure designed to recognize dogs, the lower layers recognize simple things such as outlines or color; the upper layers recognize more complex things like fur or eyes, and the upper layers define them all as a dog. Presumably speaking, the same approach can be applied to other inputs that lead a machine to teach itself. For example, it can be easily applied to the sounds that make up the words in the speech, the letters and words that form the sentences in the text, or the steering movements required to drive.

However, there are important shortcomings that current deep learning models are currently inadequate [4]. For deep learning, huge data sets are needed to train on, and these data sets must be inclusive/unbiased, and of good quality [5]. In addition, traditional deep learning requires a lot of time to train models for satisfying their purpose with an admissible amount of accuracy and relevancy [6]. Although deep learning is autonomous, it is highly susceptible to errors. Assume that an algorithm is trained with data sets small enough to not be inclusive [4]. The models trained by this way cause to irrelevant responses (biased predictions coming from a biased training set) being displayed to users [7]. One of the most important problems in artificial learning models is transparency and interpretability [8]. These artificial neural network-based models are black box models that generalize the data transmitted to it and learn from the data. Therefore, the relational link between input and output is not observable [9]. In other words, when you receive an output data against the input data, the deep learning model cannot provide the information for which reason the output is generated. The user cannot fully grasp the internal functions of these models and cannot find answers to question why and how the answers the models produce [10]. This situation creates difficulties in the application areas of these models in many aspects. For example, you stopped a taxi and got on it. The driver is such a driver that when he takes you to your destination, he turns right, turns left, and tries to get you on a strange route than you expect, but when you ask why he did so, he cannot give you a satisfactory answer. Would you be nervous? If there is no problem for you, you can ride an autonomous vehicle without a driver. As another example, when you go to the doctor, the doctor you send your complaint asks for tests and when you have those tests and send it to the doctor, the doctor tells you what your illness is. Even though he says his treatment, he does not give explanatory information about the cause of your illness. In this case, questions remain about what caused the disease and you would not be satisfied with the doctor. This is an important open point in artificial neural networks and deep learning models.

The explainable artificial intelligence (xAI) approach can be considered as an area at the intersection of several areas. One of these areas is the end user explanation section that includes social sciences. This area provides artificial intelligence to gain cognitive abilities. Another area is the human machine interface, where it can demonstrate the ability to explain; because explainable artificial intelligence needs a very high-level interaction with the user. And finally, deep learning models are an important part of an explicable artificial intelligence approach (**Figure 1**).

In this new approach, it is aimed to provide the user with the ability to explain the output data produced as well as being trained at high performance with the input data and target (class) information and tested with the new data input as in the classical machine learning models. This will create a new generation artificial intelligence approach that can establish a cause and effect relationship between input and output. It will also be the mechanism of monitoring the reliability of artificial intelligence from the user point of view. While a classic deep learning model can answer "what" or "who" questions, learning models in explainable artificial intelligence approaches can also answer "why," "how," "where," and "when" questions [10] (**Figure 2**).

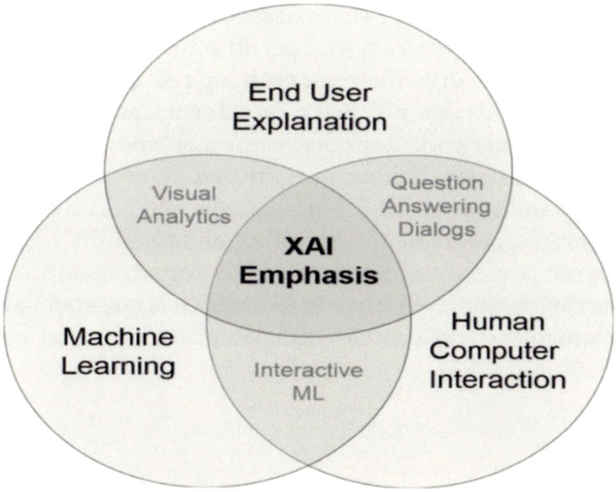

Figure 1.
Explainable artificial intelligence (xAI) [8].

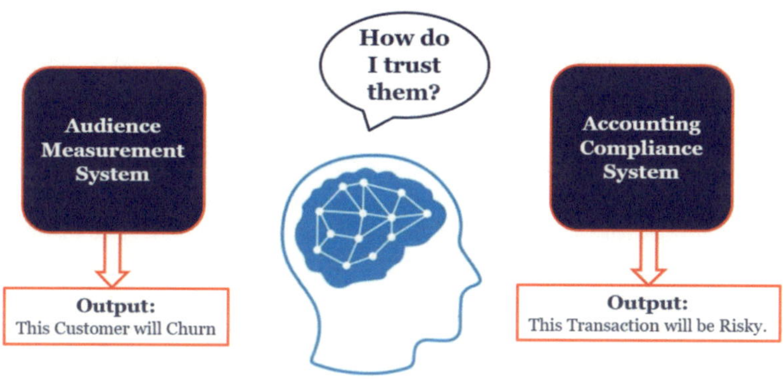

Figure 2.
How can explainable artificial intelligence (xAI) be reliable [11]?

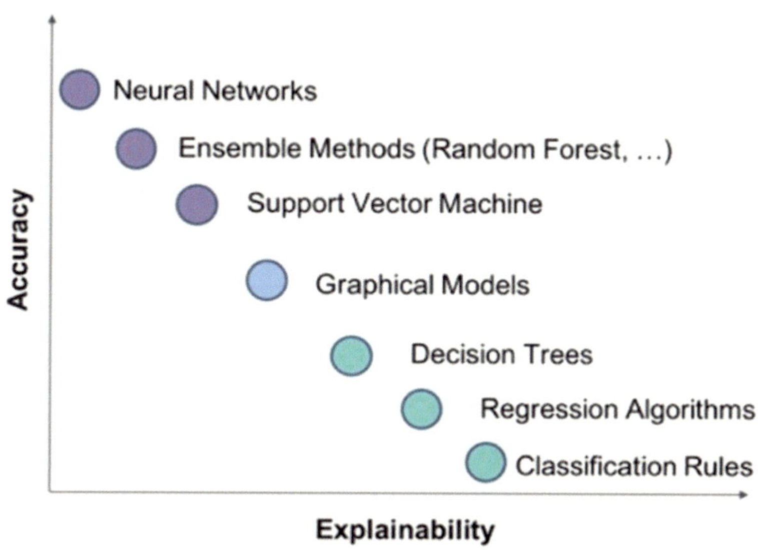

Figure 3.
Machine learning models with respect to accuracy-explainability domain [12].

Explainability and accuracy are two separate domains. In general, models that are advantageous in terms of accuracy and performance are not very successful in terms of explainability. Likewise, methods with high explainability are also disadvantageous in terms of accuracy. When methods such as classical deep learning models, artificial neural networks support vector machines are utilized, they do not give reasons why, and how their outputs created in terms of explainability. On the other hand, they are very successful in accuracy and performance. Rule-based structures, decision trees, regression algorithms, and graphical methods are good explainability but not advantageous in terms of performance and accuracy. At this point, explanatory artificial intelligence (xAI), which is targeted to be at the highest level of both explainability and accuracy and performance, reveals its importance at this point (**Figure 3**).

2. Related works

There is a transformation of machine learning that has been going on since the 1950s, sometimes faster and sometimes slower. The most studied and remarkable area in the recent past is artificial learning, which aims to model the live decision system, behavior, and responses. Successful results in the field of artificial learning led to the rapid increase of AI applications. Further studies promise to be autonomous systems capable of self-perception, learning, decision-making, and action [13].

Especially after the 1990s, although deep learning concept and foundations go back to the past, the accompanying recurrent neural networks, convolutional neural networks, deep reinforcement learning, and adversarial generative networks have achieved remarkable successes. Although successful results are obtained, these systems are insufficient in terms of explaining the decisions and actions to human users and there are limits.

The U.S. Department of Defense (DoD) explains that it is facing the challenges posed by autonomous and symbiotic systems, which are becoming smarter with each passing day. Explaining artificial intelligence or especially explanatory machine learning is important in terms of being a preview that users will encounter machines with human-like artificial intelligence in the future [14, 15]. Explained artificial intelligence is one of the Defense Advanced Research Projects Agency (DARPA) programs aimed at the development of a new generation of artificial intelligence systems, where they understand the context and environment in which machines operate and build descriptive models that enable them to characterize the real world phenomenon over time. For this purpose, DARPA recently issued a call letter for the Explainable Artificial Intelligence (XAI)—Explanatory Artificial Intelligence project [15]. Within the scope of the project, it is aimed to develop a system of machine learning techniques that focus on machine learning and human-machine interaction, and produce explanatory models that will enable end users to understand, trust, and manage emerging artificial intelligence systems. According to the researchers from DARPA, the striking successes in machine learning have led to a huge explosion in new AI capabilities that enable the production of autonomous systems that perceive, learn, decide, and act on their own. Although these systems provide tremendous benefits, their effectiveness is limited due to the inability to explain machine decisions and actions to human users.

The Explanatory Artificial Intelligence project aims to develop the machine learning and computer-human interaction tools to ensure that the end user, who depends on decisions, recommendations, or actions produced by the artificial intelligence system, understands the reason behind the system's decisions [1]. For example, an intelligence analyst who gets recommendations from big data analytics algorithms may need to understand why the algorithm advises to examine a particular activity further. Similarly, the operator, who tests a newly developed autonomous system, has to understand how he makes his own decisions to determine how the system will use it in future tasks.

The xAI tools will provide end users with explanations of individual decisions, which will enable them to understand the strengths and weaknesses of the system in general, give an idea of how the system will behave in the future, and perhaps teach how to correct the system's mistakes. The XAI project addresses three research and development challenges: how to build more models, how to design an explanation interface, and how to understand psychological requirements for effective explanations [2].

For the first problem, the xAI project aims to develop machine learning techniques to be able to manufacture explanatory models. To solve the second challenge, the program envisions integrating state-of-the-art human-machine interaction techniques with new principles, strategies, and techniques to produce effective explanations. To solve the third problem, the xAI project plans to summarize, disseminate, and apply existing psychological theory explanations. There are two technical areas in the program: the first is to develop an explanatory learning system with an explanatory model and an explanation interface; and the second technical area covers psychological theories of explanation [8].

In 2016, a self-driving car was launched on quiet roads in Monmouth County, New Jersey. This experimental tool developed by researchers at chip maker Nvidia did not look different from other autonomous cars; however, Google was different from what Tesla or General Motors introduced and showed the rising power of artificial intelligence. The car had not even followed a single instruction provided by an engineer or a programmer. Instead, it relied entirely on an algorithm that allowed him to learn to drive by watching a person driving [3]. It was an impressive success to have a car self-driving in this way. But it was also somewhat upsetting as it was not entirely clear how the car made its own decisions. The information from the vehicle's sensors went directly to a huge artificial neural network that processes the data and then delivers the commands needed to operate the steering wheel, brakes, and other structures. The results seem to match the reactions you can expect from a human driver. But what if one day something unexpected happens; hits a tree or stops at the green light? According to the current situation, it may be difficult to find the cause. The system is so complex that even the engineers who designed it can find it difficult to pinpoint the cause of any action. Moreover, you cannot ask this; there is no obvious way to design such a system that can always explain why it does what it does. The mysterious mind of this vehicle points to a vague-looking issue of artificial intelligence. Artificial intelligence technology, which is located at the base of the car and known as deep learning, has proven to be very strong in problem-solving in recent years, and this technology has been widely applied in works such as image content estimation, voice recognition, and language translation. Now the same methods can be used to diagnose lethal diseases, make million-dollar business decisions, etc. to change all industries.

Currently, the mathematical models are used to help determine who will be on parole, who will be approved to borrow money, and who will be hired. If you can access these mathematical models, it is possible to understand their reasoning. But banks, the military, employers, and others are now turning their attention to more complex machine learning approaches. These approaches can make automated decision-making completely incomprehensible. The most common of these approaches represents deep learning, a fundamentally different way of programming computers. Whether it is an investment decision or a medical decision, or a military decision, you do not want to rely solely on a "black box" method [1]. There is already a debate that it is a fundamental legal right to question a system of artificial intelligence about how it arrived at its conclusions. Starting in the summer of 2018, the European Union may require companies to provide users with an explanation of the decisions made by automated systems. This may be impossible even for systems that look comparatively simple on the surface, such as applications and Websites that use deep learning to offer advertising or song suggestions. Computers performing these services have programmed themselves and have done so in ways we cannot understand. Even the engineers who build these applications cannot fully explain their behavior.

As technology advances, we can go beyond some thresholds where using artificial intelligence in recent times requires a leap of faith. The mankind, of course, are not always able to fully explain our thought processes; but we find a variety of methods to intuitively trust people and measure them. Will this be possible for machines that think and make decisions differently than a person does? We have never built machines that operate in ways that their manufacturers do not understand. How long can we hope to communicate and deal with intelligent machines that can be unpredictable or incomprehensible? These questions take a journey toward new technology research on artificial intelligence algorithms, from Google to Apple and many other places between them, including a conversation with one of the greatest thinkers of our time.

3. Explainable artificial intelligence (xAI)

You cannot see how the deep neural network works just by looking inside. The reasoning of a network is embedded in the behavior of thousands of nerves, which are stacked and tied to tens or even hundreds of layers, mixed together. Each of the nerves in the first layer receives an input, such as the voltage of a pixel in an image, and then performs a calculation before sending a new signal as an output. This output is sent to the next layer in a complex network, and this process continues until a general output is produced. There is also a process known as back propagation that modifies the calculations of individual nerves so that a network learns to produce a desired output. Because deep learning is inherently a dark black box by nature, artificial learning models designed with millions of artificial nerve cells with hundreds of layers like traditional deep learning models are not infallible [1]. Their reliability is questioned when simple pixel changes can be seriously misleaded by causing significant deviations in the weight values in all layers of the neural network, especially in an example such as a one-pixel attack [16]. So, it becomes inevitable to ask the question of how it can succeed or fail. With the success of this type of advanced applications, its complexity also increases and its understanding/clarity becomes difficult.

It is aimed to have the ability to explain the reasons of new artificial learning systems, identify their strengths and weaknesses, and understand how they will behave in the future. For an ideal artificial intelligence system, the best accuracy and best performance, as well as the best explainability and the best interpretability are required within the cause-effect relationship. The strategy developed to achieve this goal is to develop new or modified artificial learning techniques that will produce more explicable models. These models are aimed to be combined with state-of-the-art human-computer interactive interface techniques that can be translated into understandable and useful explanation dialogs for the end user (**Figure 4**).

In this structure, unlike the classical deep learning approaches, two different elements draw attention as well as a new machine learning process. One of these

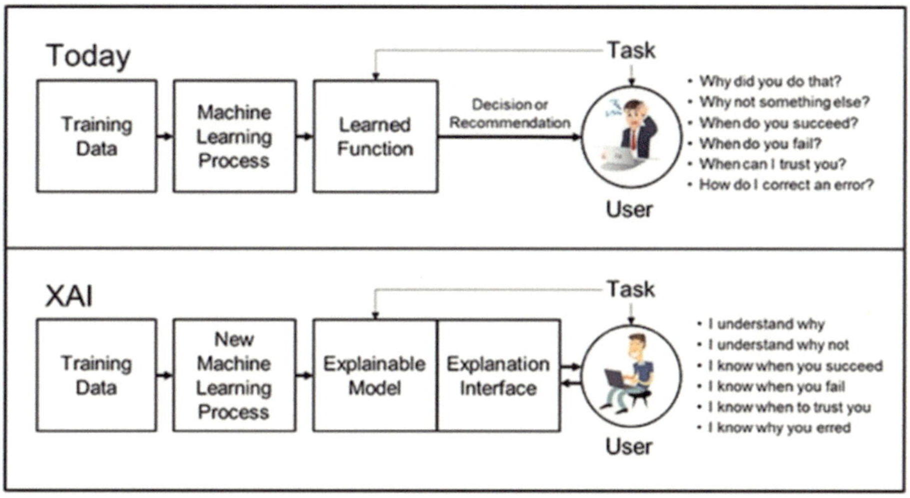

Figure 4.
Explainable artificial intelligence (xAI) project proposed by DARPA [14, 15].

is the explanatory model and the other is the explanation interface. The process of deep neural network-based machine learning is explained at the core of the artificial intelligence approach. Among the known deep learning models, autoencoder, convolutional, recurrent (LSTM), deep belief network, or deep reinforcement learning can be preferred. However, it is also possible to use a hybrid structure where several deep learning approaches are used together. Autoencoder-type model of deep neural networks are multilayered perceptron structure. In convolution neural network-type models, layers consist of convolutional layer, ReLU activation function, and max pool layer. A conventional component of the LSTM is composed of a memory cell including input, output, and forget gates. For training, the back-propagation through time algorithm can be preferred. Although the most common form of deep reinforcement learning models is deep Q network (DQN), many different variations of this model can be addressed. Many different algorithms are used as optimization algorithm. Gradient-based algorithms are the most common form of these algorithms (**Figure 5**).

Explainable model is an adaptive rule-based reasoning system. It is a structure that reveals the cause-effect relations between input data and the results obtained from the machine learning process. This causal structure learns the rules with its own internal deep learning method. In this way, the explanatory artificial intelligence model allows it to explore the causes and develop new strategies against different situations [20].

The explanation interface is a part of the user interaction. It is similar to the question-answer interface in voice digital assistants. This interface consists of a decoder that evaluates the demands of the user and an encoder unit that enables the responses from the explanatory model, which constitutes the causal mechanism of the explainable artificial intelligence, to the user (**Figure 6**).

In fact, the large networks of semantic technologies (entities) and relationships associated with Knowledge Graphs (KGs) provide a useful solution for the issue of understandability, several reasoning mechanisms, ranging from consistency checking to causal inference [21]. The ontologies realizing these reasoning procedures provide a formal representation of semantic entities and relationships relevant to a particular sphere of knowledge [21]. The input data, hidden layers, encoded features, and predicted output of deep learning models are passed into knowledge graphs (KGs) or concepts and relationships of ontologies (knowledge

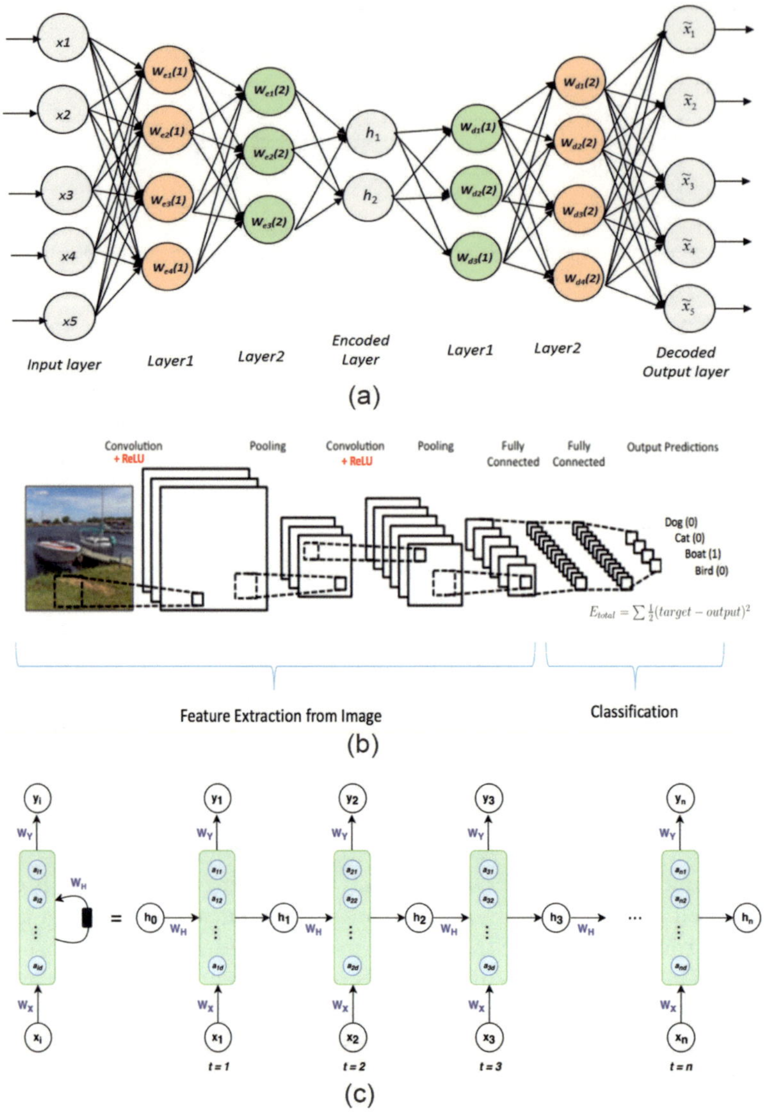

Figure 5.
Deep learning models: (a) autoencoder [17], (b) convolutional neural network [18], and (c) recurrent (LSTM) neural network [19].

matching) [21]. Generally, the internal functioning of algorithms to be more transparent and comprehensible can be realized by knowledge matching of deep learning components, including input features, hidden unit and layers, and output predictions with KGs and ontology components [21]. Besides that, the conditions for advanced explanations, cross-disciplinary and interactive explanations are enabled by query and reasoning mechanisms of KGs and ontologies [21].

Although explanatory artificial intelligence forms are of very different structures, all modules such as this explanation interface, explanatory model, and deep learning work in coordination with each other. For example, while a deep learning process estimates classes, such as the explanatory artificial intelligence model (xAI tool) developed by IBM, the concept features data obtained from this process, and another deep learning process using the same input data set produces an explanatory output for the predicted class label output [22] (**Figure 7**).

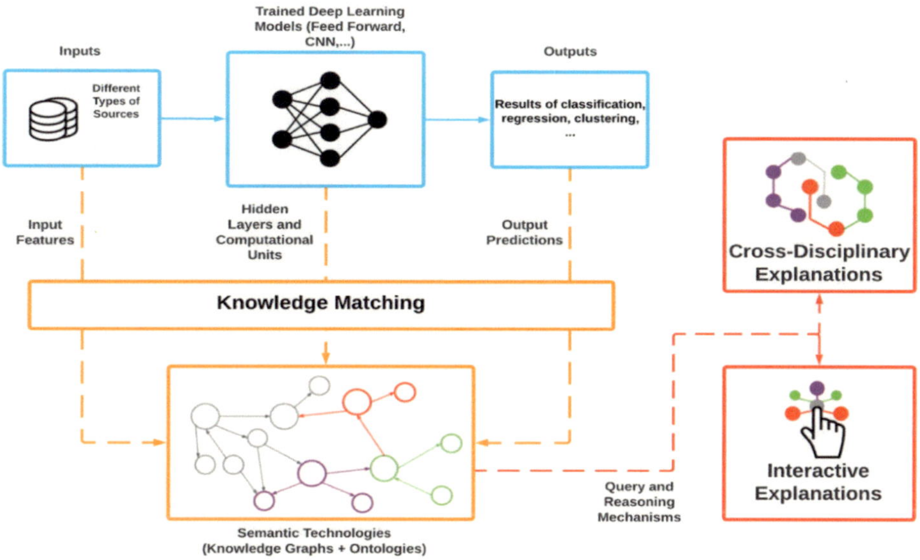

Figure 6.
Semantic knowledge matching for explainable artificial intelligence model [21].

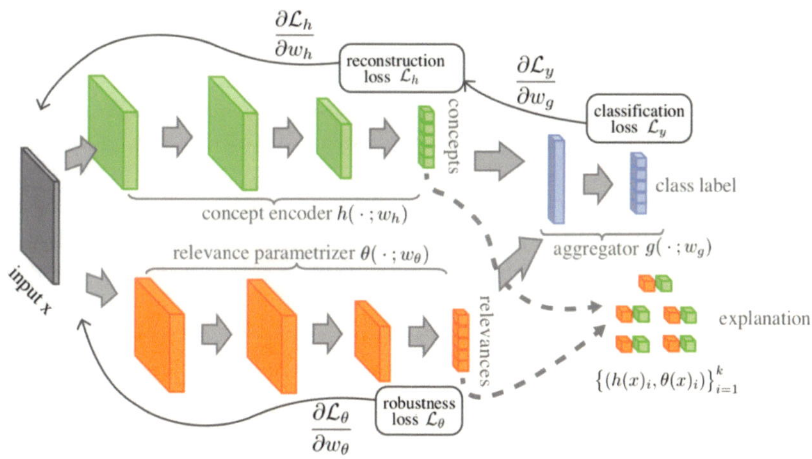

Figure 7.
Explainable artificial intelligence (xAI) tool developed by IBM [22].

At this point, the explainable artificial intelligence (xAI) tool developed by IBM is referred as a self-explaining neural network (SENN) which can be trained end-to-end with back-propagation in case of that g depends on its arguments in a continuous way [18]. The input is transformed into a small set of interpretable basis features by a concept encoder [22]. The relevance scores are produced by an input-dependent parametrizer. A prediction to be generated is merged by an aggregation function. The full model to behave locally as a linear function on h(x) with parameters θ(x), producing interpretation of both concepts and relevances, is induced by the robustness loss on the parametrizer [22]. θ(x) modeling capacity is important so that the model richness realizing higher-capacity architectures is sustained although the concepts are chosen to be raw inputs (i.e., h is the identity).

4. Meta-learning

As research and technology on machine learning progresses, artificial intelligence agents consistently display impressive learning performances that meet and exceed the cognitive skills of people in different fields. However, most AI programs are based on computing technology and even reinforcement learning (RL) models that try to regularly improve their knowledge to match human performance. By contrast, people can quickly learn new skills of new skills, simply by having a new skill [23]. The learning of the human brain so efficiently has surprised neuroscientists for years.

In traditional deep learning approaches, the system develops a data-specific model that is transmitted to it by learning from the data. The learning system will perform a certain task only for a certain environment. In the case of another environment, when a very different data is transmitted to it, this deep learning model will be insufficient to perform the task [24]. This issue reveals hard constraints in utilizing machine learning or data mining methods, since the relationship between the learning problem and the effectiveness of different learning algorithms is not yet understood. Under ideal conditions, a system should be designed in which the quality of the data given to the system differs and it can easily adapt to changes in different environments [25]. The deep learning methods used in the current situation are not successful in these situations. At this point, meta-learning, which learns to learn, is an integrated and hierarchical learning model over several different environmental models [26, 27]. As a subfield of machine learning, meta-learning learning algorithms are applied on metadata about machine learning experiments. Instead of classical machine learning approaches that only learn a specific task with single massive dataset, meta-learning is a high-level machine learning approach that learns other tasks together. Therefore, this approach requires a hierarchical structure that learns to learn a new task with distributed hierarchically structured metadata. It is generally applied for hyper parameter adjustment; recent applications have started to focus on a small number of learning. For example, if the system has already learned a few different models or tasks, meta-learning can generalize them and learn how to learn more efficiently. In this way, it can learn new tasks efficiently and create a structure that can easily adapt to changes in multiple tasks in different environments.

People are good at figuring out the meaning of a word after seeing it used only in a few sentences. Similarly, we want our ML algorithms to be generalized to new tasks, without the need for a large data set each time, and to change behavior after a few samples. In typical learning (on a single dataset), each sample targets pair functions as a training point. However, in a small number of learning situations, each "new" sample area is actually another task in itself. In other words, understanding the way that you use unique words in a particular social environment becomes a new task for your language-understanding model, and when you enter a different social environment, it means that the system can adapt to a different language-understanding model than before since it requires to dominate the words that are specific to that social environment. To make sure an ML framework can behave similarly, we have to train it on multiple tasks on its own, so we make each data set a new example of training [28] (**Figure 8**).

An alternative is to handle the task consecutively as a sequential input array and create a repetitive model that can create a representation of this array for a new task. Typically, in this case, we have a single training process with a memory or attention repetitive network [30]. This approach also gives good results, especially when the installations are properly designed for the task. The calculation performed by the

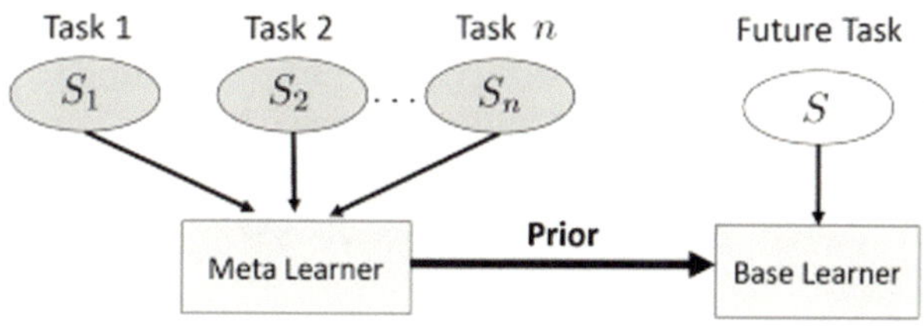

Figure 8.
Meta-learning approach [29].

optimizer during the meta-forward transition is very similar to the calculation of a repetitive network [31]. It repeatedly applies the same parameters over a series of inputs (consecutive weights and gradients of the model during learning). In practice, this means that we meet a common problem with repetitive networks. Since the models are not trained to get rid of training errors, they have trouble returning to a safe path when they make mistakes, and the models have difficulty generalizing longer sequences than those used in the order in which they were used. In order to overcome these problems, if the model learns an action policy related to the current educational situation, reinforcement learning approaches can be preferred [32] (**Figure 9**).

Formal reinforcement learning algorithm learns a policy for only single task.

$$\theta^* = \text{argmax}_\theta E_{\pi\theta(\tau)}(R(\tau)) \quad (1)$$

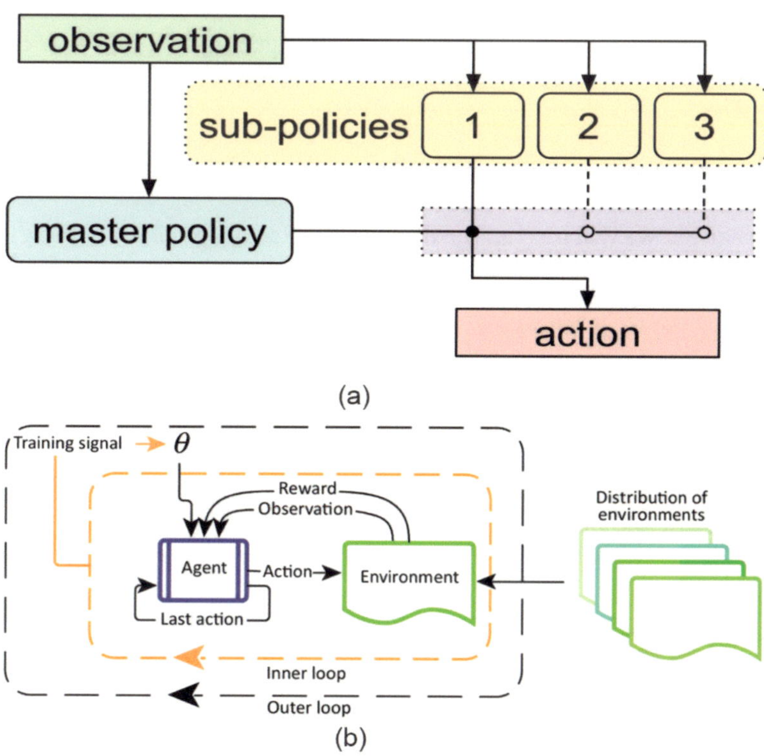

Figure 9.
(a) Meta-reinforcement learning (stack of sub-policies representation) [33] and (b) meta-reinforcement learning (inner-outer loop representation) [34].

In meta-reinforcement learning, there are two distinct processes. One of them is adaptation (inner-loop) behaving ordinary RL policy learning to produce sub-policy where $\phi_i = f_\theta(\mathcal{M}_i)$ for each environment (task) $\mathcal{M}_i$.

$$\theta^* = \text{argmax}_\theta \sum_{i=1}^{n} E_{\pi\phi_i(\tau)}[R(\tau)] \tag{2}$$

Another process is meta-training (outer-loop), which is described as meta-policy learning from all sub-policies in the adaptation process (inner-loop).

One of the main differentiers between the human brain and artificial intelligence structures such as deep neural networks, is the brain that utilizes different chemicals known as neurotransmitters to perform different cognitive functions. A new study by DeepMind believes that one of these neurotransmitters plays an important role in the brain's ability to quickly learn new topics. Dopamine acts as a reward system that strengthens connections between neurons in the brain.

The DeepMind team has used different meta-reinforcement learning techniques that simulate the role of dopamine in the learning process. Meta-learning trained a repetitive neural network (representing the prefrontal cortex) using standard deep reinforcement learning techniques (representing the role of dopamine) and then compared the activity dynamics of the repetitive network with actual data from previous findings in neuroscience experiments [27]. Recurrent networks are a good example of meta-learning because they can internalize past actions and observations and then use these experiences while training on various tasks.

The meta-learning model recreated the Harlow experiment by saying a virtual computer screen and randomly selected images, and the experiment showed that the "meta-RL agent" was learned in a similar way to the animals found in the Harlow Experiment, even when presented with the Harlow Experiment. All new images were never seen before. The meta-learning agent quickly adapted to different tasks with different rules and structures.

5. Explainable meta-reinforcement learning (xMRL)

In this section, we will discuss the development of deep reinforcement learning models with an explicable approach to artificial intelligence. Deep reinforcement learning models are machine learning models that learn what action to take according to status and reward information by maximizing reward [27]. Generally, it is widely preferred in robotic, autonomous driverless vehicles, unmanned aerial vehicles, and games. Explanatory artificial intelligence, on the other hand, provides the knowledge of why action should be taken against the situation and reward for deep reinforcement learning models. In this way, it will be possible to gain the causal decision-making ability of the model by revealing the relational links between the input and output of the developed agent (**Figure 10**).

In addition, it is possible to learn the reward derivation mechanism by using the inverse reinforcement learning model [36, 37]. In this case, unlike the previous approach, a meta-cognitive artificial intelligence model that can adapt to other environments instead of just one environment is developed [38, 39]. Taken together with the explainable artificial intelligence approach, it will be possible for the developed agent to develop his own strategy by establishing a cause-effect relationship. For example, the explainable meta-reinforcement learning agent to be developed means that in terms of meta-learning, it can learn to play Go, chess, checkers, and even learn and adapt when it is encountering a new game, and in terms of explainable artificial intelligence, it means that being aware of why it is doing any specific action against a move made by the opponent, it can explain this.

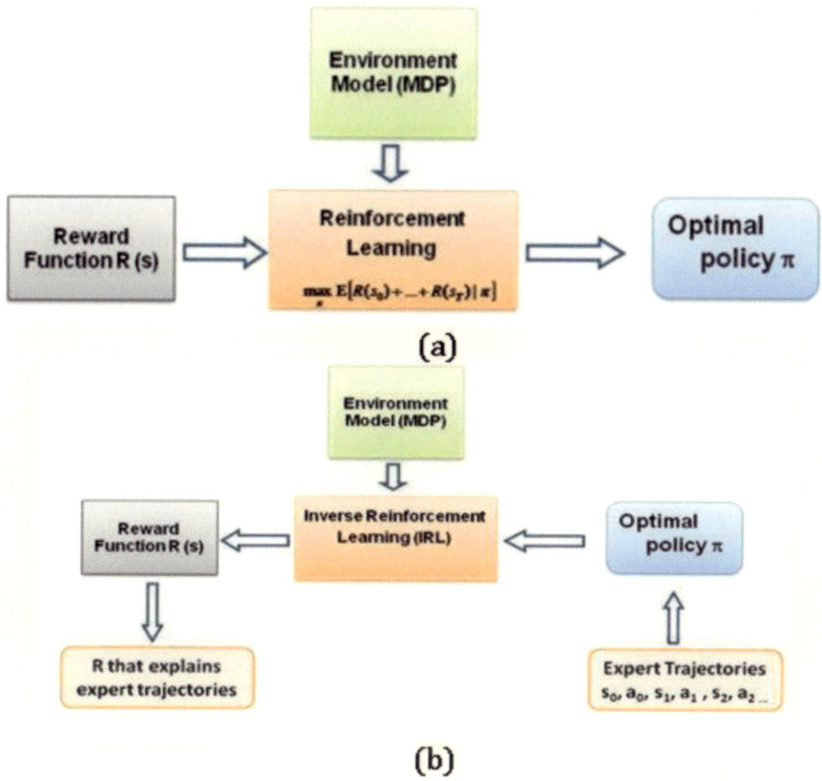

Figure 10.
(a) Reinforcement learning and (b) inverse reinforcement learning [35].

6. Discussion and concluding remarks

Next generation artificial intelligence structures are expected to have a hierarchical meta-learning ability that can adapt to many different environments, besides being a causal and explanatory power by establishing a cause-effect relationship. For this, serious effort is still needed to create flexible and interpretable models that can hold opinions from many different disciplines together and work in harmony.

We cannot ignore the advantages this will give us. For example, if we start with a medical application, after the patient data is examined, both the physician must understand and explain to the patient why he/she suggested that the explanatory decision support system suggested to the related patient that there was a "risk of heart attack." At the same time, as a meta-learning agent of this system, it has the same ability against all other diseases and it will be possible to develop appropriate treatment strategies.

While coming to this stage, what data is evaluated first is another important criterion. It is also necessary to explain what data is needed and why, and what is needed for proper evaluation. In the future, next generation deep learning and artificial intelligence forms are expected to reach the level of intelligence (singularity), which has higher performance and ability than human level. Artificial intelligence and deep learning structures mentioned in this section are thought to shed light on reaching these levels. In particular, it can be said that meta-learning approaches are capable of supporting the formation of structures that learn and adapt to multiple tasks and are also called general artificial intelligence (AGI). In the same way, it can be stated that artificial intelligence structures will help the formation of self-awareness and artificial consciousness structures based on content and causality.

Conflict of interest

The authors declare no conflict of interest.

Author details

Evren Dağlarli
Faculty of Computer and Informatics Engineering, Istanbul Technical University, Istanbul, Turkey

*Address all correspondence to: evren.daglarli@itu.edu.tr

References

[1] Adadi A, Berrada M. Peeking inside the black-box: A survey on explainable artificial intelligence (XAI). IEEE Access. 2018;**6**:52138-52160

[2] Došilović FK, Brčić M, Hlupić N. Explainable artificial intelligence: A survey. In: 2018 41st International convention on information and communication technology, electronics and microelectronics (MIPRO). IEEE; 2018. pp. 0210-0215

[3] Core MG, Lane HC, Van Lent M, Gomboc D, Solomon S, Rosenberg M. Building explainable artificial intelligence systems. AAAI; 2006. pp. 1766-1773

[4] Schnack H. Bias, noise, and interpretability in machine learning: From measurements to features. In: Machine Learning. Academic Press; 2020. pp. 307-328

[5] Huang F, Zhang J, Zhou C, Wang Y, Huang J, Zhu L. A deep learning algorithm using a fully connected sparse autoencoder neural network for landslide susceptibility prediction. Landslides. 2020;**17**(1):217-229

[6] Malik MM. A Hierarchy of Limitations in Machine Learning. 2020. arXiv preprint arXiv:2002.05193.

[7] Ahuja R, Chug A, Gupta S, Ahuja P, Kohli S. Classification and clustering algorithms of machine learning with their applications. In: Nature-Inspired Computation in Data Mining and Machine Learning. Cham: Springer; 2020. pp. 225-248

[8] Miller T. Explanation in artificial intelligence: Insights from the social sciences. Artificial Intelligence. 2019;**267**:1-38

[9] Samek W, Wiegand T, Müller KR. Explainable Artificial Intelligence: Understanding, Visualizing and Interpreting Deep Learning Models. 2017. arXiv preprint arXiv:1708.08296

[10] Fernandez A, Herrera F, Cordon O, del Jesus MJ, Marcelloni F. Evolutionary fuzzy systems for explainable artificial intelligence: why, when, what for, and where to? IEEE Computational Intelligence Magazine. 2019;**14**(1):69-81

[11] Kaushik S. Enterprise Explainable AI. 2018. Available from : https://www.kdnuggets.com/2018/10/enterprise-explainable-ai.html

[12] Dam HK, Tran T, Ghose A. Explainable software analytics. In: Proceedings of the 40th International Conference on Software Engineering: New Ideas and Emerging Results; 2018. pp. 53-56

[13] Ha T, Lee S, Kim S. Designing explainability of an artificial intelligence system. In: Proceedings of the Technology, Mind, and Society; 2018. pp. 1-1

[14] Gunning D. Explainable Artificial Intelligence (XAI). Defense Advanced Research Projects Agency (DARPA), and Web, 2; 2017

[15] Gunning D, Aha DW. DARPA's explainable artificial intelligence program. AI Magazine. 2019;**40**(2):44-58

[16] Su J, Vargas DV, Sakurai K. One pixel attack for fooling deep neural networks. IEEE Transactions on Evolutionary Computation. 2019;**23**(5):828-841

[17] Prakash PKS, Rao ASK. R Deep Learning Cookbook. Packt Publishing Ltd.; 2017

[18] Karn U. Intuitive Explanation Convolutional-Neural Networks. 2016.

Available from: https://www.kdnuggets.com/2016/11/intuitive-explanation-convolutional-neural-networks.html/3

[19] Schmidt RM. Recurrent Neural Networks (RNNs): A gentle Introduction and Overview. 2019. arXiv preprint arXiv:1912.05911.

[20] Keneni BM, Kaur D, Al Bataineh A, Devabhaktuni VK, Javaid AY, Zaientz JD, et al. Evolving rule-based explainable artificial intelligence for unmanned aerial vehicles. IEEE Access. 2019;7:17001-17016

[21] Futia G, Vetrò A. On the integration of knowledge graphs into deep learning models for a more comprehensible AI—Three Challenges for Future Research. Information. 2020;**11**(2):122

[22] Melis, D. A., Jaakkola, T. Towards robust interpretability with self-explaining neural networks. In: Advances in Neural Information Processing Systems; 2018. pp. 7775-7784

[23] Vilalta R, Drissi Y. A perspective view and survey of meta-learning. Artificial Intelligence Review. 2002;**18**(2):77-95

[24] Pfahringer B, Bensusan H, Giraud-Carrier CG. Meta-learning by landmarking various learning algorithms. In: ICML; 2000. pp. 743-750

[25] Finn C, Abbeel P, Levine S. Model-agnostic meta-learning for fast adaptation of deep networks. In: Proceedings of the 34th International Conference on Machine Learning-Volume 70. JMLR. org; 2017. pp. 1126-1135

[26] Chan PK, Stolfo SJ. Experiments on multistrategy learning by meta-learning. In: Proceedings of the Second International Conference on Information and Knowledge Management; 1993. pp. 314-323

[27] Schweighofer N, Doya K. Meta-learning in reinforcement learning. Neural Networks. 2003;**16**(1):5-9

[28] Santoro A, Bartunov S, Botvinick M, Wierstra D, Lillicrap T. Meta-learning with memory-augmented neural networks. In: International Conference on Machine Learning; 2016. pp. 1842-1850

[29] Amit R, Meir R. Meta-Learning by Adjusting Priors Based on Extended Pac-Bayes Theory. 2017. arXiv preprint arXiv:1711.01244

[30] Chan PK, Stolfo SJ. Toward parallel and distributed learning by meta-learning. In: AAAI workshop in Knowledge Discovery in Databases; 1993. pp. 227-240

[31] Vanschoren J. Meta-learning. In: Automated Machine Learning. Cham: Springer; 2019. pp. 35-61

[32] Khodak M, Balcan MFF, Talwalkar AS. Adaptive gradient-based meta-learning methods. In: Advances in Neural Information Processing Systems; 2019. pp. 5915-5926

[33] Frans K, Ho J, Chen X, Abbeel P, Schulman, J. Meta Learning Shared Hierarchies. 2017. arXiv preprint arXiv:1710.09767

[34] Botvinick M, Ritter S, Wang JX, Kurth-Nelson Z, Blundell C, Hassabis D. Reinforcement learning, fast and slow. Trends in Cognitive Sciences. 2019

[35] Jangir R. Apprenticeship Learning Using Inverse Reinforcement Learning. 2016. Available from: https://jangirrishabh.github.io/2016/07/09/virtual-car-IRL/

[36] Rakelly K, Zhou A, Quillen D, Finn C, Levine S. Efficient Off-Policy Meta-Reinforcement Learning via Probabilistic Context Variables. 2019. arXiv preprint arXiv:1903.08254

[37] Sugiyama T, Schweighofer N, Izawa J. Reinforcement Meta-Learning Optimizes Visuomotor Learning. 2020. bioRxiv

[38] Parisotto E, Ghosh S, Yalamanchi SB, Chinnaobireddy V, Wu Y, Salakhutdinov R. Concurrent Meta Reinforcement Learning. 2019. arXiv preprint arXiv:1903.02710

[39] Jabri A, Hsu K, Gupta A, Eysenbach B, Levine S, Finn C. Unsupervised curricula for visual meta-reinforcement Learning. In: Advances in Neural Information Processing Systems; 2019. pp. 10519-10530

Chapter 6

Dynamic Decision-Making for Stabilized Deep Learning Software Platforms

Soohyun Park, Dohyun Kim and Joongheon Kim

Abstract

This chapter introduces a dynamic and low-complexity decision-making algorithm which aims at time-average utility maximization in real-time deep learning platforms, inspired by Lyapunov optimization. In deep learning computation, large delays can happen due to the fact that it is computationally expensive. Thus, handling the delays is an important issue for the commercialization of deep learning algorithms. In this chapter, the proposed algorithm observes system delays at first formulated by queue-backlog, and then it dynamically conducts sequential decision-making under the tradeoff between utility (i.e., deep learning performance) and system delays. In order to evaluate the proposed decision-making algorithm, the performance evaluation results with real-world data are presented under the applications of super-resolution frameworks. Lastly, this chapter summarizes that the Lyapunov optimization algorithm can be used in various emerging applications.

Keywords: Lyapunov optimization, stochastic optimization, real-time computing, deep learning platforms, computer vision platforms

1. Introduction

Nowadays, many machine learning and deep learning algorithms have been developed in various applications such as computer vision, natural language processing, and so forth. Furthermore, the performances of the algorithms are getting better. Thus, the developments of machine learning and deep learning algorithms become mature. However, the research contributions which are focusing on the real-world implementation of the algorithms are relatively less than the developments of the algorithms themselves.

In order to operate the deep learning algorithms in real-world applications, it is essential to think about the real-time computation. Thus, the consideration of delay handling is desired because deep learning algorithm computation generally introduces large delays [1].

In communications and networks research literature, there exists a well-known stochastic optimization algorithm which is for utility function maximization while maintaining system stability. Here, the stability is modeled with queue, and then the algorithm aims at the optimization computation while stabilizing the queue dynamics. In order to formulate the stability, the queue is mathematically modeled with Lyapunov drift [2].

This algorithm is designed inspired by Lyapunov control theory, and thus, it is named to Lyapunov optimization theory [2]. In this chapter, the basic theory, examples, and discussions of the Lyapunov optimization theory are presented. Then, the use of Lyapunov optimization theory for real-time computer vision and deep learning platforms is discussed. Furthermore, the performance evaluation results with real-world deep learning framework computation (e.g., real-world image super-resolution computation results with various models) are presented in various aspects. Finally, the emerging applications will be introduced.

2. Stabilized control for reliable deep learning platforms

In this section, Lyapunov optimization theory which is for time-average optimization subject to stability is introduced at first (refer to Section 2.1), and then example-based explanation is presented (refer to Section 2.2). Finally, related discussions are organized (refer to Section 2.3).

2.1 Theory

In this section, we introduce the Lyapunov optimization theory which aims at time-average penalty function minimization subject to queue stability. Notice that the time-average penalty function minimization can be equivalently converted to time-average utility function maximization. The Lyapunov optimization theory can be used when the tradeoff exists between utility and stability. For example, it can be obviously seen that the tradeoff exists when current decision-making is optimal in terms of the minimization of penalty function, whereas the operation of the decision takes a lot of time, i.e., thus it introduces delays (i.e., queue-backlog increases in the system). Then, the optimal decision can be dynamically time-varying because focusing on utility maximization (i.e., penalty function minimization) is better when the delay in the current system is not serious (i.e., queueing delay is small or marginal). On the other hand, the optimal decision will be for the delay reduction when the delay in the current system is large. In this case, the decision should be for delay reduction while sacrificing certain amounts of utility maximization (or penalty function minimization).

Suppose that our time-average penalty function is denoted by $P(\alpha[t])$ and it should be minimized and our control action decision-making is denoted by $\alpha[t]$. Then, the queue dynamics in the system, i.e., $Q[t]$, can be formulated as follows:

$$Q[t+1] = \max\{Q[t] + a(\alpha[t]) - b(\alpha[t]), 0\} \quad (1)$$

$$Q[0] = 0 \quad (2)$$

where $a(\alpha[t])$ is an arrival process at $Q[t]$ at t when our control action decision-making is $\alpha[t]$. In (1), $b(\alpha[t])$ is a departure/service process at $Q[t]$ when our control action decision-making is $\alpha[t]$ at t.

In this section, control action decision-making should be made in each unit time for time-average penalty function minimization subject to queue stability. Then, the mathematical program for minimizing time-average penalty function, $P(\alpha[t])$ where the control action decision-making at t is $\alpha[t]$, can be presented as follows:

$$\min : \lim_{t\to\infty} \sum_{\tau=0}^{t-1} P(\alpha[\tau]) \quad (3)$$

Subject to queue stability:

$$\lim_{t\to\infty} \frac{1}{t}\sum_{\tau=0}^{t-1} Q[\tau] < \infty. \tag{4}$$

In (3), $P(\alpha[t])$ stands for the penalty function when a control action decision-making is $\alpha[t]$ at t.

As mentioned, the Lyapunov optimization theory can be used when tradeoff between utility maximization (or penalty function minimization) and delays exists. Based on this nature, drift-plus-penalty (DPP) algorithm [2–4] is designed for maximizing the time-average utility subject to queue stability. Here, the Lyapunov function is defined as $L(Q[t]) = \frac{1}{2}(Q[t])^2$, and let $\Delta(.)$ be a conditional quadratic Lyapunov function which is formulated as $\mathbb{E}[L(Q[t+1]) - L(Q[t])|Q[t]]$, which is called as the drift on t. According to [2], this dynamic policy is designed to achieve queue stability by minimizing an upper bound of our considering penalty function on DPP which is given by

$$\Delta(Q[t]) + V\mathbb{E}[P(\alpha[t])], \tag{5}$$

where V is a tradeoff coefficient. The upper bound on the drift of the Lyapunov function at t is derived as follows:

$$L(Q[t+1]) - L(Q[t]) = \frac{1}{2}\left(Q\left([t+1]^2 - Q[t]^2\right)\right. \tag{6}$$

$$\leq \frac{1}{2}\left(a(\alpha[t])^2 + b(\alpha[t])^2\right) + Q[t](a(\alpha[t]) - b(\alpha[t])). \tag{7}$$

Therefore, the upper bound of the conditional Lyapunov drift can be derived as follows:

$$\begin{aligned}\Delta(Q(t)) &= \mathbb{E}[L(Q[t+1]) - L(Q[t])|Q[t]] \\ &\leq C + \mathbb{E}[Q[t](a(\alpha[t]) - b(\alpha[t])|Q[t]],\end{aligned} \tag{8}$$

where C is a constant given by

$$\frac{1}{2}\mathbb{E}\left[a(\alpha[t])^2 + b(\alpha[t])^2|Q[t]\right] \leq C, \tag{9}$$

which supposes that the arrival and departure process rates are upper bounded. Due to the fact that C is a constant, minimizing the upper bound on DPP is as follows:

$$V\mathbb{E}[P(\alpha[t])] + \mathbb{E}[Q[t] \cdot (a(\alpha[t]) - b(\alpha[t]))]. \tag{10}$$

Algorithm 1. Stabilized Time-Average Penalty Function Minimization

Initialize:
1: $t \leftarrow 0$;
2: $Q[t] \leftarrow 0$;
3: Decision Action: $\forall\alpha[t] \in \mathcal{A}$
Time-Average Penalty Function Minimization subject to Stability
4: **while** $t \leq T$ **do** // T: operation time
5: Observe $Q[t]$;

6: $\mathcal{T}^* \leftarrow \infty$;
7: **for** $\alpha[t] \in \mathcal{A}$ **do**
8: $\mathcal{T} \leftarrow V \cdot P(\alpha[t]) + Q[t] \cdot (a(\alpha[t]) - b(\alpha[t]))$;
9: **if** $\mathcal{T} \leq \mathcal{T}^*$ **then**
10: $\mathcal{T}^* \leftarrow \mathcal{T}$;
11: $\alpha^*[t+1] \leftarrow \alpha[t]$;
12: **end if**
13: **end for**
14: **end while**

Finally, the dynamic control action decision-making $\alpha[t]$ in each unit time t for time-average penalty function $P(\alpha[t])$ minimization subject to queue stability can be formulated as follows based on the Lyapunov optimization theory:

$$\boxed{\alpha^*[t+1] \leftarrow \arg\min_{\alpha[t] \in \mathcal{A}} [V \cdot P(\alpha[t]) + Q[t] \cdot (a(\alpha[t]) - b(\alpha[t]))]} \tag{11}$$

where $\mathcal{A}$ is the set of all possible control actions and $\alpha^*[t+1]$ is the optimal control action decision-making for the next time slot.

In order to verify whether (11) works correctly or not, following two example cases can be considerable:

- *Case 1:* Suppose $Q[t] \approx \infty$. Then

$$\alpha^*[t+1] \leftarrow \arg\min_{\alpha[t] \in \mathcal{A}} [V \cdot P(\alpha[t]) + Q[t] \cdot (a(\alpha[t]) - b(\alpha[t]))] \tag{12}$$

$$\approx \arg\min_{\alpha[t] \in \mathcal{A}} [a(\alpha[t]) - b(\alpha[t])]. \tag{13}$$

Then, (13) shows that control action decision-making should works as follows, i.e., (i) the arrival process should be minimized, and (ii) the departure process should be maximized. Both cases are for stabilizing the queue, i.e., it should be beneficial when $Q[t] \approx \infty$.

- *Case 2:* Suppose $Q[t] = 0$. Then

$$\alpha^*[t+1] \leftarrow \arg\min_{\alpha[t] \in \mathcal{A}} [V \cdot P(\alpha[t]) + Q[t] \cdot (a(\alpha[t]) - b(\alpha[t]))] \tag{14}$$

$$= \arg\min_{\alpha[t] \in \mathcal{A}} V \cdot P(\alpha[t]). \tag{15}$$

Then, (15) shows that control action decision-making should work for minimizing the given penalty function. This is semantically reasonable because focusing on our main objective is possible because stability does not need to be considered because $Q[t] = 0$.

The pseudo-code of the proposed time-average penalty function minimization algorithm is presented in Algorithm 1. From line 1 to line 3, all variables and parameters are initialized. The algorithm works in each unit time as shown in line 4. In line 5, current queue-backlog $Q[t]$ is observed to be used in (11). From line 7 to line 13, the main computation procedure for (11) is described.

Up to now, the time-average penalty function minimization is considered. Based on the theory, the dynamic control action decision-making $\alpha[t]$ in each unit time t for time-average utility function $U(\alpha[t])$ maximization subject to queue stability can be formulated as follows:

$$\boxed{\alpha^*[t+1] \leftarrow \arg\max_{\alpha[t]\in\mathcal{A}} [V \cdot U(\alpha[t]) - Q[t] \cdot (a(\alpha[t]) - b(\alpha[t]))]} \tag{16}$$

where $\mathcal{A}$ is the set of all possible control actions and $\alpha^*[t+1]$ is the optimal control action decision-making for the next time slot.

2.2 Example: multicore scheduling in mobile devices

In this section, the Lyapunov optimization-based stabilized time-average optimization algorithm is introduced with one simple toy model. In this example, dynamic core allocation decision-making algorithm is designed which is for time-average energy consumption minimization subject to queue stability.

As illustrated in **Figure 1**, mobile smartphone is with the processor which is equipped with multiple cores. For example, ARM big.LITTLE processors are with multiple little and big heterogeneous cores.

In this system, the task events will be generated when users generate events, which are denoted by $a[t]$ in **Figure 1**. Then, the events will be located in the task queue (i.e., $Q[t]$ in **Figure 1**). Then, the events can be processed by the multicore processor. In this case, if many/more cores are allocated in order to process the events from the queue, the processing can be accelerated which is beneficial in terms of queue stability. However, it is not good in terms of our main objective, i.e., energy consumption minimization. On the other hand, if less cores are allocated, the processing becomes slow which is harmful in terms of queue stability but is beneficial in terms of our main objective, i.e., energy consumption minimization. Finally, the tradeoff can be observed between energy consumption minimization (i.e., our main objective) and stability. Then, it can be confirmed that Lyapunov optimization-based algorithm can be used.

In order to design the dynamic core allocation decision-making, $\alpha[t]$ in each unit time t for time-average energy consumption $E(\alpha[t])$ minimization subject to queue stability can be formulated as follows based on (11):

$$\alpha^*[t+1] \leftarrow \arg\min_{\alpha[t]\in\mathcal{A}} [V \cdot E(\alpha[t]) + Q[t] \cdot (a(\alpha[t]) - b(\alpha[t]))] \tag{17}$$

where $\mathcal{A}$ is the set of all possible core allocation combinations and $\alpha^*[t+1]$ is the optimal core allocation decision-making for the next time slot. Here, it is obvious

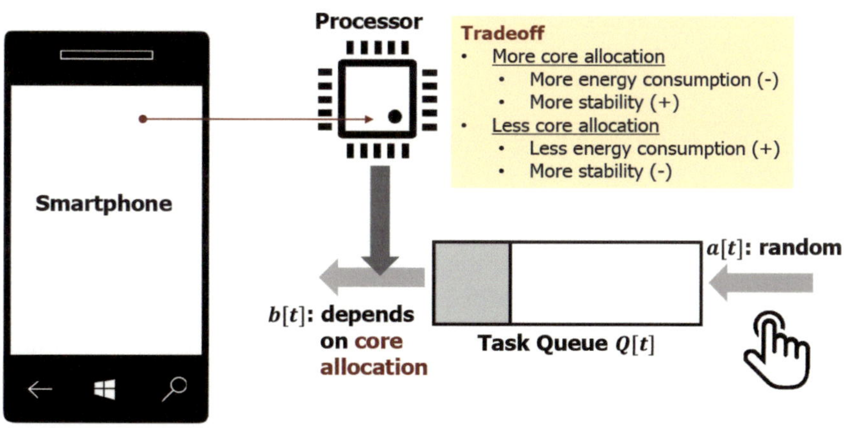

Figure 1.
Mobile devices with multicore processors.

that the arrival process is not controllable (i.i.d. random events); thus, it can be ignored. Then, the final form of the dynamic decision-making algorithm can be defined as follows:

$$\alpha^*[t+1] \leftarrow \arg\min_{\alpha[t]\in\mathcal{A}} [V \cdot E(\alpha[t]) - Q[t] \cdot b(\alpha[t])]. \tag{18}$$

In order to check whether the derived Eq. (18) is correct or not, two example cases can be considered, i.e., (i) $Q[t] \approx \infty$, and (ii) $Q[t] = 0$:

- *Busy queue case* ($Q[t] \approx \infty$): in this case

$$\alpha^*[t+1] \leftarrow \arg\min_{\alpha[t]\in\mathcal{A}} [V \cdot E(\alpha[t]) - Q[t] \cdot b(\alpha[t])], \tag{19}$$

$$= \arg\min_{\alpha[t]\in\mathcal{A}} [-b(\alpha[t])] = \arg\max_{\alpha[t]\in\mathcal{A}} b(\alpha[t]), \tag{20}$$

Thus, the departure process should be accelerated, i.e., more cores should be allocated. This is semantically true because the fast processing events from the queue is desired if overflow situations happen.

- *Busy queue case* ($Q[t] = 0$): In this case

$$\alpha^*[t+1] \leftarrow \arg\min_{\alpha[t]\in\mathcal{A}} [V \cdot E(\alpha[t]) - Q[t] \cdot b(\alpha[t])], \tag{21}$$

$$= \arg\min_{\alpha[t]\in\mathcal{A}} V \cdot E(\alpha[t]), \tag{22}$$

Thus, less cores should be allocated for energy consumption minimization which is our main objective. This is semantically true because the given main objective should be desired if the system is stable, i.e., $Q[t] = 0$.

As discussed with examples, the proposed Lyapunov optimization-based dynamic core allocation decision-making algorithm works as desired.

2.3 Discussions in stabilized control

The proposed dynamic super-resolution model selection algorithm is beneficial in various aspects, as follows.

2.3.1 Hardware/system-independent self-adaptation

Suppose that this proposed algorithm is implemented in supercomputer-like high-performance computing machines. In this case, the processing should be fast; thus, the queue-backlog is always low. Therefore, the system has more chances to focus on our main objective, i.e., penalty function minimization or utility function maximization. On the other hand, if the hardware itself is performance/resource limited (e.g., mobile devices), then the processing speed is also limited due to the low specifications in processors. Thus, the queue-backlog can be frequently busy because it may not be able to process many data with the queue even though it utilizes the fastest model. Therefore, it can be finally observed that the proposed algorithm is self-adaptive which can adapt depending on the given hardware/system specifications. It automatically adapts the models based on the given hardware/system; thus, it does not require system engineer's trial-and-error tuning.

Furthermore, the proposed algorithm is reliable according to the fact that the self-adaptation is for maximizing its *utility* while maintaining *stability*.

2.3.2 Low-complexity operation

As shown in Algorithm 1, the computation procedure is iterative for solving closed-form equation, i.e., (11) and (16). Thus, the computational complexity of the proposed algorithm is polynomial time, i.e., $O(N)$, where N is the number of the given control actions. Thus, it guarantees low-complexity operations.

3. The use of Lyapunov optimization for deep learning platforms

As explained, the Lyapunov optimization theory is a scalable, self-configurable, low-complexity algorithm which can be used in many applications. In this section, the use of Lyapunov optimization for deep learning and computer platforms is discussed in two different ways, i.e., departure process control (refer to Section 3.1) and arrival process control (refer to Section 3.2). Finally, its related performance evaluation results are presented (refer to Section 3.3).

3.1 Lyapunov control over departure processes

As illustrated in **Figure 2**, stabilized real-time computer vision platforms should be equipped with queues in order to handle bursty traffics. If the queue is busy or near-overflow, the departure process should be accelerated. Thus, the simplest model should be used for reducing the corresponding computation. On the other hand, if the queue is empty, deep learning computation accuracy can be improved with more sophisticate models because we have enough time to conduct the computation. Thus, multiple models are desired in order to select one depending on queue backlog.

In **Figure 2**, multiple models exist, and it can be seen that the simplest model (i.e., low-resolution model) is able to conduct fast computation, but it presents low learning accuracy. On the other hand, the most sophisticate model (i.e., high-resolution model) is good for accurate learning performance, but it introduces computation delays. Thus, the tradeoff exists between performance and delays, i.e.,

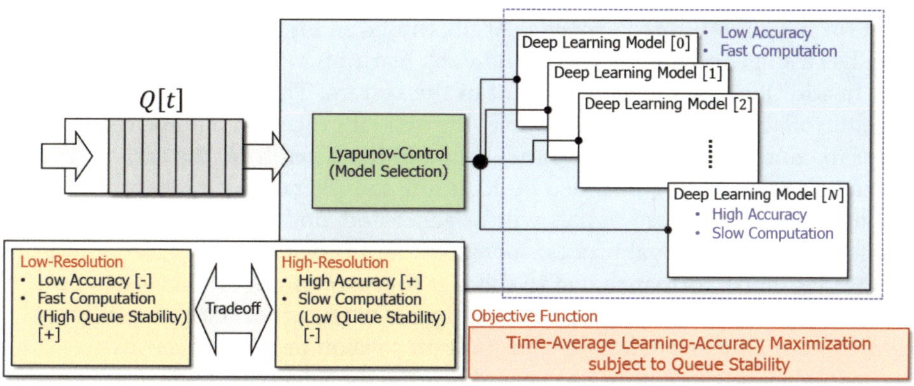

Figure 2.
Lyapunov control over departure processes in real-time computer vision platforms for time-average learning accuracy maximization subject to queue stability.

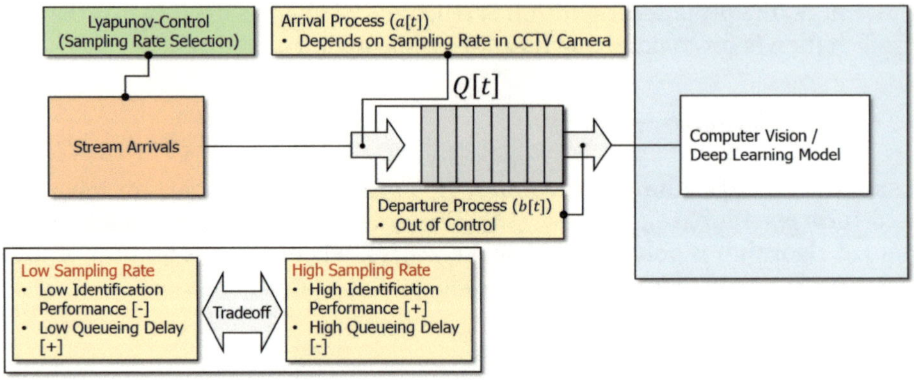

Figure 3.
Lyapunov control over arrival processes in real-time computer vision platforms for time-average learning accuracy maximization subject to queue stability.

Lyapunov optimization theory-based dynamic model selection decision-making algorithm can be designed as follows:

$$\alpha^*[t+1] \leftarrow \arg\max_{\alpha[t]\in\mathcal{A}} [V \cdot A(\alpha[t]) - Q[t] \cdot (a(\alpha[t]) - b(\alpha[t]))] \tag{23}$$

and this can be reformulated as follows due to the fact that the arrival process is out of control:

$$\alpha^*[t+1] \leftarrow \arg\max_{\alpha[t]\in\mathcal{A}} [V \cdot A(\alpha[t]) + Q[t] \cdot b(\alpha[t])] \tag{24}$$

where $A(\alpha[t])$ stands for the learning-accuracy when the model selection decision is $\alpha[t]$ at t. Here, $\mathcal{A}$ is the set of all possible deep learning models, and $\alpha^*[t+1]$ is the optimal control action decision-making for next time slot.

3.2 Lyapunov control over arrival processes

The stabilized real-time computer vision platform in Section 3.1 is novel and scalable; however it has burden because multiple deep learning models should be implemented in a single platform.

Thus, a new dynamic control algorithm with a single deep learning model is also needed for resource-limited systems. As illustrated in **Figure 3**, our considering system has a single computer vision and deep learning model in computing platforms. In addition, the queue is in front of the system. Thus, the departure process is not controllable anymore. In this case, the arrival process should be controllable in order to control the queue dynamics for stability. Therefore, the arrival image/video streams should be controlled by handling sample rates. If high-frequency sampling is available, more signals will be generated, and then the results will be enqueued. Thus, the arrival process increases. This is beneficial because it increases computer vision performance due to the fact that more images/videos can be obtained especially in surveillance applications. On the other hand, i.e., if low-frequency sampling is conducted, the computer vision performance can be degraded, whereas the number of arrival process data decreases which is beneficial in terms of stability. Eventually, the tradeoff between computer vision performance and delays can be observed. Finally, Lyapunov optimization theory-based sampling rate selection decision-making algorithm can be designed as follows:

$$\alpha^*[t+1] \leftarrow \arg\max_{\alpha[t] \in \mathcal{A}} [V \cdot A(\alpha[t]) - Q[t] \cdot (a(\alpha[t]) - b(\alpha[t]))] \tag{25}$$

and this can be reformulated as follows due to the fact that the departure process is out of control:

$$\alpha^*[t+1] \leftarrow \arg\max_{\alpha[t] \in \mathcal{A}} [V \cdot A(\alpha[t]) - Q[t] \cdot a(\alpha[t])] \tag{26}$$

where $A(\alpha[t])$ stands for the learning accuracy when the sample rate selection decision is $\alpha[t]$ at t. Here, $\mathcal{A}$ is the set of all possible sample rates, and $\alpha^*[t+1]$ is the optimal control action decision-making for next time slot.

3.3 Performance evaluation and discussions

In this section, the performance evaluation results of the proposed algorithm in Section 3.1 are presented. The data-intensive simulation-based evaluation is performed, and then the results are presented in **Figure 4**. In addition, **Table 1** shows the performance of super-resolution depending on the number of hidden layers. If the number of hidden layers is maximum (i.e., 20 in this research), the PSNR and structural similarity (SSIM, one of the widely used performance metrics in super-resolution) values are maximum. However, the computation times (for CPU-only and CPU-GPU) become slow.

As illustrated in **Figure 4**, if the models are static (i.e., *deep* or *shallow*), the curves show that the two models are not efficient. The deep model cannot handle the overflow situations; thus, the queue diverges. On the other hand, the shallow

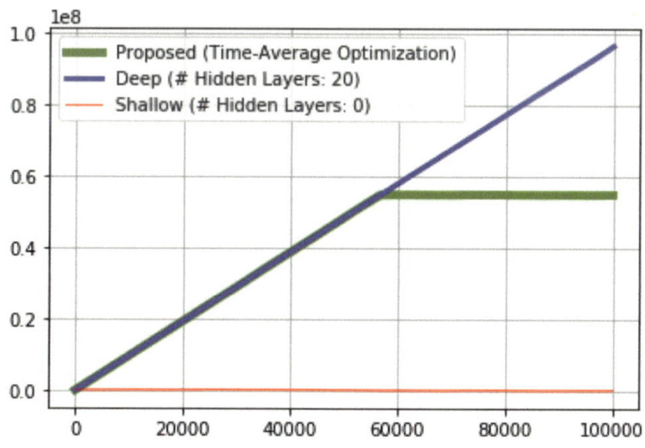

Figure 4.
Performance evaluation: Queue-backlog (x-axis, unit time; x-axis, queue occupancy (unit: Bits)).

Depth (# of hidden layers)	0	4	6	8	11	14	17	20
PSNR (dB)	30.400	32.560	33.010	33.229	33.379	33.435	33.495	33.523
SSIM	0.8682	0.9100	0.9160	0.9180	0.9200	0.9200	0.9210	0.9220
Processing time (CPU − only)	0.0020	0.3210	0.5468	0.7725	0.9940	1.3170	1.6220	1.9600
Processing time (CPU + GPU)	0.0010	0.0100	0.0120	0.0152	0.0189	0.0224	0.0262	0.0305

Table 1.
Tradeoff between utility and delay obtained from super-resolution performance measurement results (processing time have measured on 512 × 768 images).

model is too fast; thus, the queue is always empty. This is obviously positive for stability where the performance in terms of super-resolution performance is the lowest. Thus, it might be better if the algorithm allows certain amounts of delays in order to enhance the quality of super-resolution. The proposed algorithm is initially follows *deep* model because the queue is idle during the initial phases. If the queue becomes filled with certain amounts of images (i.e., near threshold), it starts the control, i.e., self-adaptive, near the unit time of 5800. Thus, the proposed algorithm starts to select super-resolution models which can handle delays. Thus, it is true that the proposed algorithm is better than the other two static algorithms.

For the proposed self-adaptive stabilized algorithm, the evaluation with two processing capabilities (CPU-only platform vs. CPU-GPU platform), it can be observed that the CPU-GPU platform selects the maximum performance super-resolution model (i.e., 20 hidden layers in **Table 1**) 4.36 times more than the CPU-

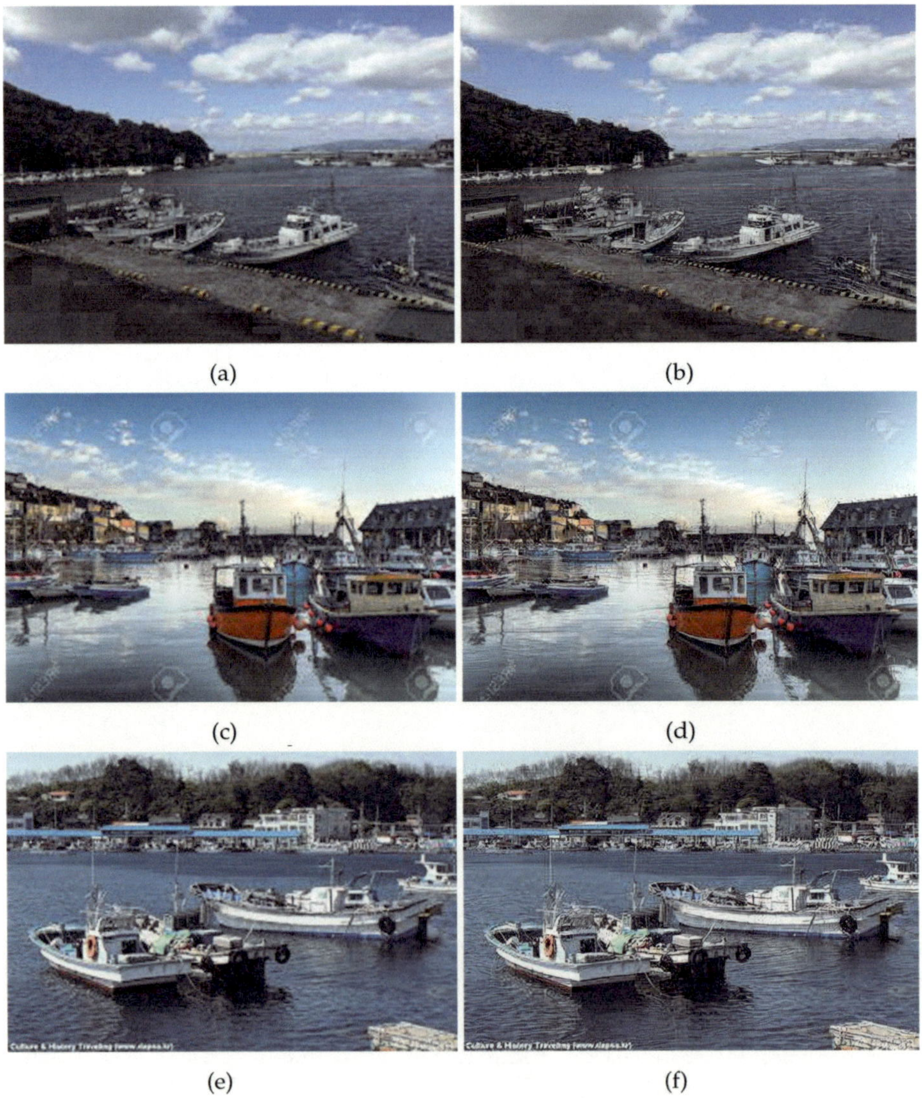

Figure 5.
Super-resolution computation results. Note that the model for low-resolution is bicubic which has no hidden layers. (a) Image #1 (low-resolution), (b) image #1 (high-resolution), (c) image #2 (low-resolution), (d) image #2 (high-resolution), (e) image #3 (low-resolution) and (f) image #3 (high-resolution).

only platform. It means that the proposed algorithm is self-adaptive depending on the hardware/platform requirements. This is obviously beneficial in terms of system engineers because they do not need to conduct trial-and-error-based system parameter tuning anymore.

In order to confirm the performance of super-resolution models, **Figure 5** shows the super-resolution computation results with real-world images. As can be seen in the figures, the super-resolution models show better performances if they have more hidden layers, as shown in **Figure 5b**, **Figure 5d**, and **Figure 5f**. For the super-resolution computation without hidden layers, this paper uses bicubic interpolation, as shown in **Figure 5a**, **Figure 5c**, and **Figure 5e**. Finally, these results show that our considering Lyapunov control algorithms for adaptive deep learning platforms can make different super-resolution performance depending on queue-backlog size information.

4. Emerging applications

As presented, the Lyapunov optimization framework is for time-average utility maximization while achieving queue stability; and this theory is scalable; thus it is widely applicable [2]. Therefore, there exist many applications based on this algorithm as follows.

4.1 Adaptive video streaming

Kim et al. [3, 5] design a dynamic control algorithm for time-average streaming quality (i.e., peak-signal-to-noise ratio (PSNR)) maximization subject to transmit buffer stability in wireless video networks. Koo et al. [6, 7] also propose a novel dynamic adaptive streaming over HTTP (DASH)-based mechanism for video streaming quality maximization under the consideration of battery status, LTE data quota, and stability in hybrid LTE and WiFi networks.

4.2 Networks

Neely et al. [8] proposed a novel dynamic multi-hop routing algorithm which is for energy-efficient data/packet forwarding in wireless ad hoc and sensor networks subject to queue stability.

4.3 Security applications: surveillance monitoring

Mo et al. [9] design a deep learning framework for CCTV-based distributed surveillance applications. In the system, multiple deep learning frameworks exist; and each deep learning model is with its own configurations. In this situation, there exists a tradeoff between complexity and performance. Therefore, the proposed CCTV-based surveillance algorithm adaptively selects a deep learning model depending on queue-backlog in the system for recognition performance maximization subject to CCTV queue stability. Kim et al. [10] also design a novel face identification deep learning frameworks for CCTV-based surveillance platforms. Instead of having multiple deep learning models, this system has one learning system (based on OpenFace open-source software library) and controls the sampling rates of the CCTV camera. Finally, the proposed decision-making algorithm dynamically selects CCTV sampling rates for recognition performance maximization subject to CCTV queue stability.

4.4 Others

The application of Lyapunov optimization-based dynamic control algorithm for dynamic reinforcement learning policy design is illustrated in [11]. In addition, the adaptive control algorithms using the Lyapunov optimization framework in stock market pricing and smart grid are introduced in [12, 13].

5. Conclusions

This chapter introduces a dynamic control decision-making algorithm, inspired by Lyapunov optimization theory under the situation where the tradeoff between utility/performance and delays exists. Thus, the dynamic decision-making algorithms aim at time-average utility maximization (or penalty minimization) in real-time deep learning platforms. As discussed, the Lyapunov optimization-based algorithms are scalable, hardware/system-independent, self-configurable, and low-complexity. Thus, it can be used in various emerging applications such as video streaming, wireless networks, security applications, and smart grid applications.

Acknowledgements

This work is supported by the National Research Foundation of Korea (2019R1A2C4070663, 2019M3E4A1080391). J. Kim is a corresponding author (e-mail: joongheon@korea.ac.kr).

Conflict of interest

The authors declare no conflict of interest.

Author details

Soohyun Park[1], Dohyun Kim[2] and Joongheon Kim[1*]

1 Korea University, Seoul, Republic of Korea

2 Naver Webtoon Corporation, Seongnam, Republic of Korea

*Address all correspondence to: joongheon@korea.ac.kr

References

[1] Kim D, Kwon J, Kim J. Low-complexity online model selection with Lyapunov control for reward maximization in stabilized real-time deep learning platforms. In: Proceedings of the IEEE International Conference on Systems, Man, and Cybernetics (SMC '18); 7–10 October, 2018; Miyazaki, Japan: IEEE; 2018. pp. 4363-4368

[2] Neely M. Stochastic Network Optimization with Application to Communication and Queueing Systems. Vermont, USA: Morgan & Claypool; 2010

[3] Kim J, Caire G, Molisch A. Quality-aware streaming and scheduling for device-to-device video delivery. IEEE/ACM Transactions on Networking. 2016;**24**:2319-2331. DOI: 10.1109/TNET.2015.2452272

[4] Choi M, Kim J, Moon J. Adaptive detector selection for queue-stable word error rate minimization in connected vehicle receiver design. IEEE Transactions on Vehicular Technology. 2018;**67**:3635-3639. DOI: 10.1109/TVT.2017.2776327

[5] Kim J, Meng F, Chen P, Egilmez H, Bethanabhotla D, Molisch A, et al. Demo: Adaptive video streaming for device-to-device mobile platforms. In: Proceedings of the ACM International Conference on Mobile Computing and Networking (MobiCom '13), 30 September–4 October, 2013; Miami, FL, USA: IEEE; 2013

[6] Koo J, Yi J, Kim J, Hoque M, Choi S. REQUEST: Seamless dynamic adaptive streaming over HTTP for multi-homed smartphone under resource constraints. In: Proceedings of the ACM International Conference on Multimedia (MM '17), 23–27 October, 2017; Mountain View, CA, USA: IEEE; 2017

[7] Koo J, Yi J, Kim J, Hoque M, Choi S. Seamless dynamic adaptive streaming in LTE/Wi-fi integrated network under smartphone resource constraints. IEEE Transactions on Mobile Computing. 2019;**18**:1647-1660. DOI: 10.1109/TMC.2018.2863234

[8] Neely M. Energy optimal control for time varying wireless networks. IEEE Transactions on Information Theory. 2006;**52**:2915-2934. DOI: 10.1109/TIT.2006.876219

[9] Kim J, Mo YJ, Lee W, Nyang D. Dynamic security-level maximization for stabilized parallel deep learning architectures in surveillance applications. In: Proceedings of the IEEE Symposium on Privacy-Aware Computing (PAC '07); 1–3 August, 2017; Washington DC, USA: IEEE; 2017. pp. 192-193

[10] Kim D, Kim J, Bang J. A reliable, self-adaptive face identification framework via Lyapunov optimization. In: Proceedings of ACM Symposium on Operating Systems Principles (SOSP) AI Systems Workshop (AISys '17), 28 October, 2017; Shanghai, China: ACM; 2017

[11] Neely M, Supittayapornpong S. Dynamic Markov decision policies for delay constrained wireless scheduling. IEEE Transactions on Automatic Control. 2013;**58**:1948-1961. DOI: 10.1109/TAC.2013.2256682

[12] Neely M. Stock market trading via stochastic network optimization. In: Proceedings of IEEE Conference on Decision and Control (CDC '10), 15–17 December, 2010; Atlanta, GA, USA: IEEE; 2010

[13] Neely M, Tehrani A, Dimakis A. Efficient algorithms for renewable energy allocation to delay tolerant consumers. In: Proceedings of IEEE International Conference on Smart Grid Communication (SmartGridComm '10), 4–6 October, 2010; Gaithersburg, MD, USA: IEEE; 2010